IMAGES of America

PLYMOUTH

On the Cover: This is the farmhouse of John and Gertrude Theis, located near where Vicksburg Lane and Rockford Road intersect today. This late-19th-century photograph also features the couple's sons, Hubert and Peter, who each held their own adjoining farms just south of Turtle Lake. (Courtesy of the Plymouth Historical Society.)

IMAGES
of America

PLYMOUTH

Sarah Winans and Natasha Thoreson
Foreword by Jeff Wosje

ARCADIA
PUBLISHING

ISBN 978-1-4671-0423-4

Published by Arcadia Publishing
Charleston, South Carolina

Printed in the United States of America

Library of Congress Control Number: 2019940788

For all general information, please contact Arcadia Publishing:
Telephone 843-853-2070
Fax 843-853-0044
E-mail sales@arcadiapublishing.com
For customer service and orders:
Toll-Free 1-888-313-2665

Visit us on the Internet at www.arcadiapublishing.com

*This book about Plymouth's past is dedicated
to those who shape its future.*

Contents

FOREWORD

Plymouth has a rich history that includes its original inhabitants, the Dakota, as well as early traders, settlers, town organizers, and businesspeople. Seeing the history of our community chronicled is important, gratifying, and unifying.

As Plymouth is capturing the past through this book, community leaders are preparing for the future. Knowing where we have been makes it easier to chart our path forward. As we look ahead, we build on the strong foundation established by those who came before us. We seek to create a future that expands on today's successes and promotes innovation, collaboration, and community.

Innovation—Plymouth is home to 60,000 jobs and is a technology and med-tech hub. Plymouth will continue to nurture its reputation as a place where companies invest, innovate, and thrive. Continued outreach helps us understand and provide what businesses need. Fortifying our businesses helps build a stronger community that benefits from a diversified economic base and ample employment opportunities.

Collaboration—for decades, Plymouth has emphasized collaboration. The City of Plymouth, school districts, other government agencies, private sector businesses, civic groups, and individuals have come together to build safe, strong neighborhoods, protect our environment, develop a nationally accredited park and recreation system, and support our highly regarded schools. Continuing to seize opportunities to work together will ensure efficiency, avoid duplication of effort, and maximize resources.

Community—as this book is published, Plymouth is a city of approximately 77,000 residents. While Plymouth has grown significantly during the past few decades, we have placed a priority on creating amenities, events, and facilities that bring us together. In the future, nurturing a sense of community will remain a priority as we continue to foster an environment where all are respected, valued, and connected.

Our future community is inescapably shaped by our past. Fortunately, past planning and current successes have positioned us for a bright future. On behalf of the City of Plymouth, thank you to Sarah Winans and Natasha Thoreson for recording our history and making this book possible. Knowing our shared history deepens connections to our community and one another.

—Jeff Wosje
Mayor of the City of Plymouth

Acknowledgments

Driving down Fernbrook Lane in Plymouth, one might notice the little white building nestled in a city park not far from a hockey rink and wonder about its story. It is worth taking the time to wonder because inside this unassuming building, Plymouth's old town hall, is the story of a sleepy little township that grew into a progressive and diverse city. That story and the walls that contain them have been preserved thanks to the unwavering efforts of the Plymouth Historical Society. This book has as its foundation the society's archives, newsletters, and narratives. In particular, we would like to thank Bob Gasch for grounding our research in the larger context of Minnesota history and Ted Hoshal for sharing his carefully researched resources related to Plymouth and Medicine Lake.

Though he is with us in spirit only, many thanks are owed to longtime Plymouth Historical Society member Gary Schiebe. For 30 years, until his untimely passing in 2017, Gary worked tirelessly for the organization. A gifted storyteller, Gary's stories are preserved in decades' worth of society newsletters, in narratives woven together over half a lifetime. He was also responsible for collecting many of the images used in this book.

Unless otherwise noted, all images in this book appear courtesy of the Plymouth Historical Society. They were scanned with help from volunteers Aradhana Dalai and Rajarajeswari Kamaraj on equipment purchased with a generous gift from the Plymouth Lions Club. We also wish to thank the following individuals and organizations for the remaining images: Brian Rosemeyer and Helen LaFave at the City of Plymouth, Hennepin County Library, Alyssa Thiede and Cara Letofsky at the Hennepin History Museum, Becky Herke, Howard Hunt, Genevieve Ernst Lane, Medicine Lake History Collection, Minnesota Historical Society, Aaron Isaacs at the Minnesota Streetcar Museum, Debra Bertrand Palmquist, Lorelie Batula at the Plymouth Fire Department, Joel Franz at the Plymouth Police Department, Pam Schmitt at St. Joseph's Community Parish, Wayzata Historical Society, West Hennepin County Pioneer Association, and Verl Raap at the Zuhrah Shriners.

INTRODUCTION

Mystery is essential to any good historical tale, and it is a mystery that defines the story of Plymouth's name. In the United States, 30 cities, villages, towns, and townships are named Plymouth, most likely in honor of Plymouth Colony, now Plymouth, Massachusetts. Founded by the Pilgrims in 1620, Plymouth's legacy is celebrated each November at Thanksgiving, though the 17th-century event bore little in common with the modern holiday. As the Pilgrims' Plymouth holds such importance to the history of the country, it makes sense that the colonial town inspired the name of Plymouth, Minnesota. On the other hand, as Jonas Howe, Plymouth's first clerk, noted, "unless on the principle of opposites," there seemed to be no reason that "a town settled by Catholics and Agnostics should bear the name of the town settled by the people who came over on the Mayflower."

Years before Minnesota became a state, hopeful land speculators designed a plan for a town they named Plymouth to be built on the northwest shore of Parkers Lake. Streets were named Alpha, Beta, Gamma, and so forth, though building along those streets was slow. The town initially consisted of a gristmill, moved from Wayzata, and small homes built for the mill hands. Unfortunately, a flood in 1857 destroyed the fledgling pioneer town. The mill was moved to St. Anthony, along with the industrial opportunity it afforded. But settlers continued to arrive, establishing homesteads across the 36 square miles of Township 118.

In April 1858, the year Minnesota became a state, Hennepin County Commissioners christened Township 118 "Plymouth," presumably after the failed Parkers Lake settlement. The township, as a unit of local government, was required to organize. On May 11, 1858, Francis Day hosted open elections for town offices at his home. Day's home being too small to accommodate the turnout, the meeting was adjourned to Charles Farrington's home. Francis Huot, Daniel Parker, and Francis Gorham were elected town supervisors, Jonas Howe was elected clerk, Francis Day became the town's assessor, Charles Tolman the collector, Eustache Boucher the overseer of the poor, Phillip Otto and Alfred Jordan, the town constables, and Francis Clay and William Karson the justices of the peace.

Here is where the mystery begins. Less than a month later, on June 1, 1858, the town met again and, after considerable discussion, voted to change Plymouth's name to Medicine Lake. No recorded reason exists for the name change, though the name itself refers to the township's largest lake. Even stranger, no one really knows why Medicine Lake is called Medicine Lake.

According to the earliest history of Plymouth, the name Medicine Lake derived from a Dakota legend. In this story, a man in his canoe was capsized by a sudden storm. His body could not be found, his spirit lost to the lake. This "lake of the spirit," or *Mde Wakan* in the Dakota language, was mispronounced as "Medicine" by the English.

A 1940s-era story claims that the Mdewakanton Dakota offered settlers the word "medicine" as the equivalent to their tribal name. The Dakota understood "medicine" to mean something that was spiritual. This, they felt, approximated the meaning of Mdewakanton, "those who were born of the lake of the spirit." The "lake of the spirit" referred to is not Medicine Lake, but Mille Lacs in northeast Minnesota.

The truth likely falls somewhere in between. The lake was probably named for the Mdewakanton people who camped upon its shores. "Mdewakanton," a word that would have been unfamiliar to most of Plymouth's settlers, was presumably bastardized as "Medicine."

Medicine Lake, as the name for Township 118, was only used once. The call for the next town meeting, held on April 5, 1859, was issued in the name of Medicine Lake. But, for unknown reasons, it was never used again. All subsequent town meeting notes referred to the town of Plymouth and that is how it was recognized by county officials. Some speculate that the voters originally dissatisfied with the name Plymouth lacked sufficient influence to effectuate the name change. Others believe it was simply an error in completing the proper paperwork. No matter the case, why Plymouth remained "Plymouth" remains a mystery.

Today, Plymouth, Minnesota is the largest of the nation's 30 Plymouths and the seventh-largest city in Minnesota. It is home to over 60,000 jobs, many in the medical and technical industries. Global-minded corporations such as Honeywell, Cargill, and Medtronic attract employees from all over the world. Still, Plymouth's largest employer is Wayzata Public Schools. Education has long been a priority for Plymouth. In 1892, the town clerk, Jonas Howe, explained that Plymouth's "inhabitants are nearly all farmers and fully convinced that the best stock is the schoolhouse; the best cultivators yet invented are school teachers; the best security for free government is intelligent voters. And although many of us do not boast of much learning, we fully realize that knowledge is power and are not disposed to withhold the money necessary to educate our children." Today, the reputation of local schools attracts families from all over the Twin Cities metropolitan area seeking high-quality education for their children.

Opportunities like these have spurred Plymouth's tremendous growth in recent years. Located just 12 miles from downtown Minneapolis, the close-knit farming community of Plymouth managed to maintain its rural roots through the early 1970s. Urbanization slowly commenced as Plymouth shed its township status in 1955. The first strip mall, Plymouth Shopping Center, was built in the 1950s. The sewer system began development in 1966. The village's first water tower was erected in 1970. Roads continued to be paved through the early 1970s. Plymouth installed its first traffic light in 1972, signaling the rapid development that was to follow.

Plymouth reflects a newly diverse and dynamic American suburb where industrial, residential, and recreational areas converge. This book aims to bridge Plymouth's past with its present, connecting the city's newest pioneers with those who founded it so many years ago.

One

Plymouth's First Settlers 1850–1870

The Dakota people were the first to inhabit the land now known as Plymouth. They traveled between a series of seasonal encampments depending on the resources available at each. In its natural state, much of Plymouth was covered by a dense growth of maple, oak, and elm trees emerging from fertile clay loam. Here and there, the trees parted to reveal a marsh or lake, providing the habitat for a diverse range of plants and animals. The land provided the Dakota with opportunities to fish, hunt, trap, farm, and harvest maple sugar, acorns, and wild rice.

In 1851, two years after the establishment of the Minnesota Territory, the Dakota signed the Treaty of Traverse des Sioux and the Treaty of Mendota, ceding nearly 24 million acres of land to the US government. These treaties, along with the expansion of pre-emption rights to include unsurveyed lands, spurred an influx of white settlement. It also was another step in the increasing dispossession of Dakota land, leading to the US–Dakota War of 1862.

Plymouth's initial settlers came from places close to home (Canada, New England, the Midwest) and far (England, Ireland, Germany, Scandinavia). Like the Dakota, these immigrants were attracted to the rich abundance of the land. It did not take long for these early settlers to divide Plymouth's expanse into roughly 80 homesteads, transforming the big woods into furrowed fields dotted with square-hewn cedar and tamarack log cabins.

According to the 1860 US Census, over 400 settlers lived in Plymouth, most having arrived before 1857. The following chapter details their images and stories as preserved through family histories and the records of the Plymouth Historical Society.

The Treaty of Traverse des Sioux of 1851, depicted here in this sketch by Frank B. Mayer, was a contract between the Sisseton and Wahpeton bands of Dakota and the US government. It transferred ownership of large portions of southern and western Minnesota from the Dakota to the United States, thus opening the door for settlers. (Courtesy of the Minnesota Historical Society.)

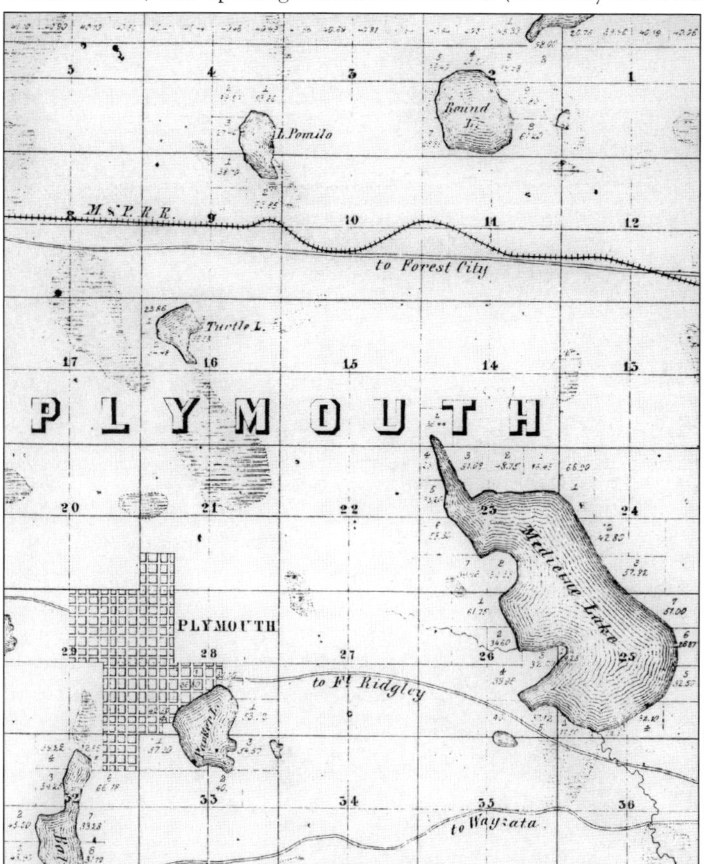

This map shows the settlement of Plymouth planned for the northwest shore of Parkers Lake. Although the land had already been claimed by Daniel Parker, George Butler, and Amos Hoyt, a gristmill was erected near the water, along with small cabins for the mill hands. The mill was in operation for less than six months before it flooded and was moved to St. Anthony.

Antoine LeCounte, Plymouth's first settler, made his claim on the east shore of Medicine Lake in October 1853. LeCounte was born near the Red River in 1822. His father, known as "Antoine LeGros," was a guide, explorer, and trader. Antoine often accompanied him on his travels. This changed in 1838 when Antoine joined LeGros on a tragic expedition with a man named Thomas Simpson. (Courtesy of St. Joseph's Parish Community.)

LeGros agreed to lead Simpson along a dangerous shortcut through the wilderness. On the fourth day, Simpson shot LeGros. Before succumbing to his wounds, LeGros urged his son to flee. Antoine and another guide, the frontiersman Pierre Bottineau (pictured), returned to bury LeGros's body. Years later, LeGros's mummified body was exhibited throughout the state before it was revealed as a hoax, the body a convincing plaster creation. (Courtesy of the Minnesota Historical Society.)

Many of Plymouth's earliest land claims were made at the Forest City, Greenleaf, or St. Anthony land office (pictured). These land offices were established by the territorial government to support new arrivals to the area. Settlers registered their claims at the nearest office, sometimes traveling with their neighbors. (Courtesy of the Minnesota Historical Society.)

The extended Parker family was among Plymouth's first residents. Daniel Parker, wife Hester, daughter Harriet, father James, and mother Deborah left Maine to meet Daniel's brothers Alfred, Charles, and Israel, who had claimed land in Minnesota. In Illinois, they boarded a steamboat, where Deborah died of cholera. At first, Daniel was not impressed by Minnesota, but he agreed to stay, becoming the town's first supervisor and chairman.

Francis and Matilda Clay registered a claim on September 1, 1854, and built a log cabin near Gleason Lake. Francis volunteered for the Civil War, while Matilda served as postmistress. She embraced social activities and wrote to friends "of having gone to a ball in a coach and four." She failed to mention that the "coach" was a bobsled and the "four" were Francis and three men who pulled it.

Andrew Jordan (pictured at center) brought his family by covered wagon to Minnesota Territory in 1855. He built a small cabin on the southwest shore of Jordan Lake, which was later drained. When Minnesota became a state in 1858, Jordan was appointed the town's first constable. Jordan hosted Sunday morning Mass in his home, providing accommodations for the traveling Catholic priest from Saturday until Monday.

In August 1862, the citizens of Plymouth met to discuss methods for raising its quota of soldiers. The following resolution was adopted unanimously: "We, the citizens of Plymouth, believe it to be the duty of every man to sustain the government in her present emergency, either in men or money, and we pledge ourselves as a town to furnish our quota, if it can be done, by appealing to the patriotism of her citizens, believing we are second to none in the love of our country and purity of patriotism." The town pledged $25 to every volunteer who enlisted from Plymouth. Two of those volunteers were Karl and John Jordan (pictured). The brothers were born in Germany and came to the United States with their parents in 1852. Karl perished in the war in 1862 at the age of 22. Two years later, John enlisted in the 8th Minnesota Volunteer Regiment. At the end of his service, he returned to Plymouth, married Mary Anna Weidenbach, raised 12 children, and served as the town clerk for over 20 years.

James and Elizabeth Hughes settled briefly in Iowa before embarking to Minnesota Territory in a covered wagon in March 1854. Their journey began with six yoke of oxen and two cows. Spring snowstorms made travel perilous, and James left the wagon in search of food for his family. They arrived in Plymouth in May 1854 with only five oxen and one cow. James later served as a blacksmith at Fort Snelling during the Civil War. The Hughes' family history contains many stories of encounters with the Dakota, who had established trails throughout the area. One encounter describes difficulty in communication between a group of Dakota and Elizabeth as she worked a quilting frame. In another story, James provides first aid to a Dakota man with frozen feet. Later that winter, the man left a saddle of venison at the Hughes' cabin door.

James Hughes's brother Charles was 15 when he arrived in Plymouth with his parents in 1853. Before enlisting in the military, Charles ran a carriage shop in St. Anthony. During the Civil War, he participated in over 21 battles, sending letters of his experiences to his sister. Charles then joined General Sully's march up the Yellowstone River. He returned to Plymouth in 1865 and purchased 40 acres of his own.

This c. 1860 photograph shows Samuel Merchant's cabin. Merchant filed his homestead claim in September 1854 and moved his family to the cabin in May 1855. The Merchant family later replaced this cabin with a large wooden frame farmhouse whose attic unwittingly housed the earliest town records—ones believed to be lost—until they were serendipitously discovered over 100 years later.

Originally from Germany, Peter Winnen arrived in Plymouth with his parents in 1855. Though ostensibly a farmer, Peter preferred wood carving. He roamed the woods, studying nature for ideas to use in his designs. Winnen became well-known for his carvings, including several elaborate pulpits and a much-photographed rustic footbridge that crossed the creek below Minnehaha Falls. (Courtesy of the Western Hennepin County Pioneer Museum.)

To make time for woodcarving, Winnen taught his nine daughters to run the farm, which included a berry patch. One day at market, a man noted that the berry business was profitable, but it was difficult to find workers to pick the fruit. Peter laughed, "Oh, I have nine and all made to order." The Winnen daughters were savvy entrepreneurs who foraged for ginseng to buy ribbons and dresses.

Christopher and Efrosene Sandhoff traveled from Germany in 1862 to join sons Herman and Charles in Plymouth. Christopher met Napoleon in Berlin in 1812, agreeing to help haul French army provisions en route to Russia. He was 75 years old when he boarded a ship for America, the ship's captain toasting his intrepid spirit with a glass of wine. Christopher purchased land east of what became Mt. Olivet Cemetery.

Herman Sandhoff registered his 160 acres on June 6, 1856. A stonesman by trade, Herman worked on several buildings in St. Anthony while also maintaining his farm along the northern edge of Medicine Lake. He eventually expanded his farm to 285 acres. He married Amelia on February 26, 1863, and they had seven children.

In the 1850s, missionaries came a few times a year to lead church services. Herman and Amelia Sandhoff hosted services in their log home. The services were followed by large dinners. Amelia loved music, and it is easy to imagine the role music might have played in these celebrations. Later, services were moved to the District 51 schoolhouse and then to the home of Christopher Sandhoff.

The Herman Sandhoff family soon replaced their log cabin with an impressive farmhouse. It was a story-and-a-half structure with two additions that eventually totaled 74 feet in length. After Herman's death, the house was split in two, and one half was moved to make two separate homes for relatives.

According to the family's history, Charles Smith, brother of Amelia Smith Sandhoff, was stationed at Fort Hutchinson during the Civil War. Charles received a furlough to attend Amelia and Herman's wedding on February 26, 1863. After the ceremony, on his long journey back to the fort, Charles contracted pneumonia and died. He was brought home to be buried on the farm. With no clergy available, the Smiths' neighbor Jonas Howe conducted the funeral.

At age 11, Peter Rascop Jr. came from Germany with his parents and sisters. The Rascops settled in Chicago but moved to Minnesota to escape a cholera epidemic. On October 8, 1860, Peter's father claimed 160 acres. Peter served in the Civil War. According to the family history, of the 200 men in his company, Peter was one of 20 who survived. He married his wife, Susan, on February 3, 1866.

Thomas Ditter boarded a ship in Germany bound for America in 1859. During the voyage, he met the Lawrence Adelman family, including the Adelmans' daughter Rosa. In 1863, Thomas enlisted to fight in the Civil War. After the war, he looked up the Adelman family, who had settled in Minnesota. Thomas and Rosa married in 1873 and bought a farm in Plymouth in 1883. They had 11 children and were members of St. Joseph's Church, to which the family donated a stained-glass window. Thomas owned a livery barn in Minneapolis with his partner Mr. Kees. He was also skilled in the construction trade, which he put to use in the planning and construction of Plymouth's original town hall in 1885. Built adjacent to a corner of his farm, the town hall was located near Plymouth Creek, shown here in this photograph of his daughter Katherine.

It is believed that Joseph Day, his mother, and some of his siblings arrived in Plymouth in 1865, having taken the same train that carried Abraham Lincoln's body to Illinois. Joseph's farm was located at what is today the corner of Highway 55 and Fernbrook Lane. He was a skilled carpenter and helped build the first Methodist church at Parkers Lake. He also owned one of the area's first steam threshers, which he shared during harvest with his neighbors.

This photograph, taken in August 1915, shows Ferdinand Boucher and his family seated in front of their home. Though thoroughly modern, the left portion of this house was most likely raised around the original log cabin built by Ferdinand's father, Eustache, upon his arrival in Plymouth. Once a month, beginning in 1856, Mass was held at the Bouchers' log cabin. This group of mostly French-Canadian settlers eventually formed the St. Joseph's Parish Community. (Courtesy of St. Joseph's Parish Community.)

James, Thomas, and John Francis Rooney (pictured together) were the sons of James and Bridgett Rooney. The Rooneys claimed 80 acres in Plymouth Township and 80 acres in Medina Township on April 3, 1856. Bridgett, James Sr., and their eldest daughter Mary Ann lived in a covered wagon on the land until their log cabin was completed. In their early 20s, James Jr. and John Francis purchased a farm together in Minnetonka, while Thomas stayed on the family farm. Their youngest sister, Eliza (pictured alone), was born in 1868. The Rooney family history captures the uncertainty and fear felt no doubt by all in Minnesota in 1862 as the US–Dakota War unfolded.

Originally from England, Frank and Mary Ann Hatcher paid $1.25 an acre for their farm on March 3, 1857. The Hatcher family history recounts that they preferred to make the two-day walk to Minneapolis for supplies "with a sack of flour on their backs," rather than the three-day trip with oxen and the wagon.

Immigrants from Germany, brothers Frank and Ferdinand Kreatz claimed their farms on October 1, 1860, at the Forest City land office. Both married and had families. Ferdinand's son Gustav moved with the family from their original log cabin to their farmhouse at the age of nine months. He never left, spending his entire life on the family farm. He married Jennie Hatcher, daughter of Frank and Mary Ann Hatcher.

Frederick Radintz left Germany at the age of 24 seeking adventure. After arriving in New York, he worked in a Michigan coal mine before deciding to move to Australia. Before boarding a ship in New York, he heard about a yellow fever epidemic and headed to Chicago instead. In Chicago, a coworker died of cholera, and Frederick was on the move again, this time to St. Anthony. He arrived in Plymouth in 1854 and claimed land on November 24, 1860, perhaps having had enough adventure. His wife, Christina, came to America at 19, hoping to live "where children could always have plenty to eat." She worked for politician A.M. "Major" Fridley in St. Anthony. Fridley gifted a wedding dress and a cow when she married Frederick in 1857. The Radintz family history tells of a large Dakota camp at Gleason Lake in the 1850s.

Carl and Johanna Schiebe came with their family to the United States in 1863. They lived with their three children, Charles, Gustave, and Mary, in New York City for three years before moving to Minneapolis. In 1873, the Schiebes purchased 40 acres and the Farmer's Home Hotel and moved to Plymouth. In 1879, Carl bought another 160 acres.

Fredericka Sprung Schiebe came to the United States at age 14 in 1867. She married Charles on April 23, 1873. She loved to garden, a passion that provided both beautiful flowers and vegetables for the family's hotel. She also was enamored by the stars and loved to study them. Fredericka and Charles had 15 children.

Dennis Schmitz, shown here with his wife, Susan, arrived in Plymouth in 1855 and selected a heavily wooded 160 acres. He registered his land at Forest City on November 22, 1860, along with Francis Day, Henry Smith, and Jonas Howe. He set to work building a house with the abundant timber. The family history describes the process. A pit was dug, and rollers were placed across it. Then, a log was laid upon the rollers, and a man in the pit used a cross-cut saw as it rolled across. Of course, great effort was also required to clear fields for planting crops. Chopping down trees was followed by the arduous task of "grubbing," or removing the stumps. (Below, courtesy of the Minnesota Historical Society.)

Katherine Spurzem Mengelkoch came to America in the early 1850s. She worked in a St. Paul hotel, where she met Clemens Mengelkoch. Katherine helped many women during childbirth. Clem paid cash for his land in 1856, the "Abstract of Lands" for Hennepin County incorrectly listing his name as "Chas. Meryelhook." The Mengelkochs also built commercial property featuring apartments and shops on Fourth Street and Plymouth Avenue in Minneapolis.

Jacob and Catherine Mengelkoch acquired their Plymouth homestead in 1860. The original District 95 log schoolhouse was on land adjacent to the northeast corner of the Mengelkoch farm. The Mengelkochs were a hospitable family, often providing accommodations for farmers traveling to Minneapolis. They were known for hosting barn dances and house parties, adding joy to the routine of farm life.

Jonas Howe was born in Massachusetts and trained as a painter before arriving in Minnesota Territory in 1854. Jonas facilitated town meetings and held several offices in Plymouth, including clerk and justice of the peace, in addition to serving as a member of the Minnesota House of Representatives. He was an abolitionist and served with the Minnesota Volunteer Infantry during the Civil War. He helped organize the National Grange and the founding of the State School for the Deaf at Faribault. Besides being a civic leader, Jonas's legacy is preserved through his art. A few of his paintings survive in the collection of the Hennepin History Museum. *Artist's Paradise* is an example of his interpretation of Minnesota scenery. Jonas was also a frequent contributor to *Farm, Stock and Home*, an agricultural publication. He died in 1898 and was buried at Parkers Lake Cemetery. (Below, courtesy of the Hennepin History Museum.)

Jonas Howe was instrumental in the founding of the Minnesota State School for the Deaf in Faribault in 1863. His daughter Cora was in the school's first graduating class. The Howe family's commitment to education was evident in many ways, from their support of the local school to their willingness to share books with neighbors. (Courtesy of the Minnesota Historical Society.)

In 1873, the original Howe family log cabin burned and was replaced by this farmhouse. Many Howe family adventures were captured in the memoirs of Jonas Howe's daughter, Annie "Nannie" Estella Howe Best. Best, who attended the University of Minnesota and became a teacher, chronicled anecdotes of interactions between her Plymouth neighbors and experiences such as surviving a tornado.

According to Nannie's memoir, the Howes organized a literary society with the help of the school teacher, Miss Campbell. At the winter meetings, Jonas read Shakespeare, his wife Margaret Adele told stories, and Miss Campbell recited poetry. Nannie's sister Laura Howe, pictured here, wrote original poetry, including a poem that won a $50 prize.

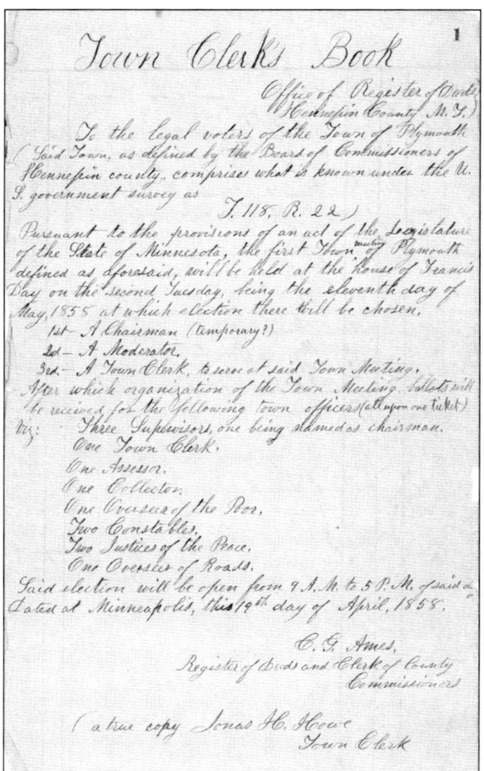

Town Clerk's Book 1

Office of Register of Deeds
Hennepin County M. T.)

To the legal voters of the Town of Plymouth (Said Town, as defined by the Board of Commissioners of Hennepin county, comprises what is known under the U. S. government survey as T. 118, R. 22)

Pursuant to the provisions of an act of the Legislature of the State of Minnesota, the first Town meeting of Plymouth defined as aforesaid, will be held at the house of Francis Day on the second Tuesday, being the eleventh day of May, 1858 at which election there will be chosen,

1st - A Chairman (temporary?)
2d - A Moderator.
3rd - A Town Clerk, to serve at said Town Meeting.

After which organization of the Town Meeting ballots will be received for the following town officers (all upon one ticket) viz:

Three Supervisors, one being named as chairman.
One Town Clerk.
One Assessor.
One Collector.
One Overseer of the Poor.
Two Constables.
Two Justices of the Peace.
One Overseer of Roads.

Said election will be open from 9 A.M. to 5 P.M. of said day.
Dated at Minneapolis, this 19th day of April, 1858.

C. G. Ames,
Register of Deeds and Clerk of County Commissioners

(a true copy Jonas H. Howe
Town Clerk

Jonas Howe recorded the first entry in the Town Clerk's Book on April 19, 1858. At this meeting, it was decreed that township elections would be held on May 11, 1858. Francis Huot was the chairman of the meeting, and George Messinger served as the moderator. The action was approved by C.G. Adams, clerk of county commissioners.

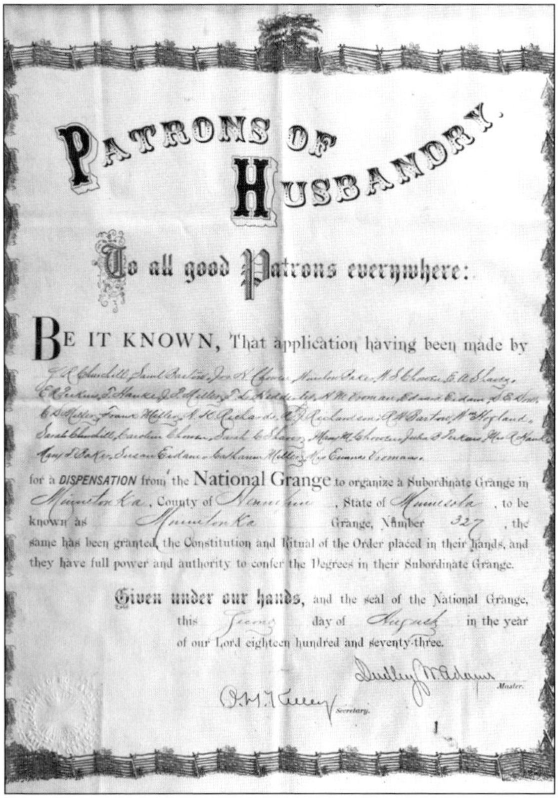

PATRONS OF HUSBANDRY.

To all good Patrons everywhere:

BE IT KNOWN, That application having been made by [illegible]

for a *DISPENSATION* from the National Grange to organize a Subordinate Grange in Minnetonka, County of Hennepin, State of Minnesota, to be known as Minnetonka Grange, Number 327, the same has been granted, the Constitution and Ritual of the Order placed in their hands, and they have full power and authority to confer the Degrees in their Subordinate Grange.

Given under our hands, and the seal of the National Grange, this [illegible] day of August in the year of our Lord eighteen hundred and seventy-three.

Dudley W. Adams, Master.

O. H. Kelley, Secretary.

Howe was a key figure in the creation of the National Grange of the Order of Patrons of Husbandry, working with founder Oliver Hudson Kelley. The Grange endeavored to educate farm families, to support agricultural colleges, and to advocate for related policies. Howe lectured for the Grange in many Minnesota communities. In 1883, a combined meeting of the Minnehaha, Minneapolis, Plymouth, and Minnetonka Granges was held, with Howe offering a popular resolution applauded energetically by attendees. (Courtesy of the West Hennepin County Pioneer Museum.)

Jonas Howe, polymath that he was, helped haul timbers for the Hennepin Avenue Bridge, believed to be the first permanent structure to span the Mississippi River. The 620-foot suspension bridge opened on January 23, 1855, with great festivity, including a mile-long procession of 61 sleighs and a speech by Minnesota territorial governor Willis Gorman. (Courtesy of the Minnesota Historical Society.)

Two

Early Days in the Township 1870–1900

When land developers first designed the town of Plymouth on the northwest shore of Parkers Lake, they mapped out a main street. This was to be the heart of Plymouth, its downtown. Unbeknownst to all, a flood in 1857 would change the look of the town forever. The town plan abandoned, the township instead grew as a series of homesteads connected by informal roads, wagon trails, and footpaths.

The neighboring cities of Wayzata, Robbinsdale, and Medina all retain the 19th-century charm and history of their downtown districts. These districts succeeded when Plymouth's did not because they were chosen as the sites for railroad stops and stations. The first railway to creep west from St. Anthony bypassed Plymouth township, stopping in Wayzata instead. Fifteen years later, a second railway built a flag stop in the Medina neighborhood of Hamel. Thanks to the natural dynamism and energy afforded by a railroad stop, businesses in these areas flourished.

Instead, Plymouth grew from two distinct points that still define the city today. The first of these points is the intersection of Highway 55 and Old County Road 15, known for nearly 100 years as Schiebe's Corner. Schiebe's Corner still serves as a transportation crossroads; today, it is the site of the Station 73 Park & Ride.

Plymouth's second important point of growth is at the very center of the city. The first town hall was built on the edge of the marsh that, today, connects Plymouth Creek Center with the Millennium Garden and Plymouth Creek Park. The site was chosen for the town hall in 1885 because it was as near to the center of the township as could be, a nod to the democratic principles that the country was founded on. No one person had to travel further than another to vote or attend town meetings.

This area still marks the city's civic heart. Plymouth's "downtown" can be found just west of the old town hall along the stretch of Plymouth Boulevard between Highway 55 and Rockford Road. Here, Plymouth residents can access the city hall, post office, and library along with other city amenities such as the Hilde Performance Center, Ice Arena, and Lifetime Fitness.

This chapter focuses on the town's initial phase of development and the people who helped shape its earliest landscape.

The Farmer's Home Hotel was built by Nicholas Bofferding in 1863 and sold to Carl Schiebe in 1872. Schiebe expanded the number of rooms, added barns, and built an icehouse. The outdoor dance floor was so popular that it was enclosed to extend the fun throughout winter. For 50¢, a couple could dance all afternoon and evening. Schiebe's Corner, as it became known, tied early Plymouth to communities both west and east.

This 1885 photograph titled "The Boys at Schiebe's" reflects the popularity of Schiebe's Corner and its importance as a stopover for travelers. The Schiebe family worked the fields and hotel themselves, with much of the food served coming from their farm. On a typical day, over 50 pies were baked. Guests paid 25¢ for a meal, and there was a saloon for men and a wine room for women.

Another part of early downtown Plymouth was Edward Reinke's blacksmith business, a convenient location for farmers making the two day trip to Minneapolis. The travelers could spend the night at Schiebe's Corner and have their horses shod or their wagons repaired just down the street. The c. 1908 photograph includes Edward Sr., Edward Jr. (7), Otto (5), Minnie (12), and Anna (10).

Until 1917, the Reinke home, a one-and-a-half story house built upon a flagstone foundation, was just a few blocks from Schiebe's Corner. As a result of a land dispute, the Reinke family purchased 15 acres of land along what is now County Road 73, and the house was pulled by horses to this new location. Take note of Edward's wife, Henriette, sitting in the window behind the children.

Plymouth's first school opened in 1858 and was known as District 95. The first building was a 14-by-14-foot log cabin, and the first teacher, Lorinda Shaw, was paid $28 per month. The school housed around 26 students, ranging in ages from 5 to 19 years old. Some students walked up to three miles to attend school. In 1869, Gertrude Howe (pictured left, at left) became the teacher. Members of the school board included Clem Mengelkoch, Jacob Mengelkoch, Nicholas Bofferding, and Jonas Howe. As enrollment grew, so did the need for a larger schoolhouse. In 1872, Clem Mengelkoch was awarded the building contract with a budget of $600. A wood-frame building with desks, a well, and blackboards was constructed. Records show additional expenses of 35¢ for a broom and 40¢ for matches and a dipper.

In 1893, Alice Creelman gifted her sister Alma with a diary "to write something every day." Thirteen-year-old Alma followed this prescription, capturing her daily life as she sewed mittens, completed lessons, and "snowballed" with friends. She told of taking a train to the Minneapolis Public Library and skiing to school. Her descriptions of winter include horses belly-deep in snow and bundling up so much "that I [al]most smothered!"

School attendance was impacted by the weather and the need for students' help on family farms. On February 1, 1893, student Alma Creelman wrote of how there were "only eleven scholars at school today" due to extreme cold and snowfall. She continued, "[The snow] drifted so last night we did not think we was going to school. But when we saw teacher going we thought we could go if she could." (Courtesy of the Minnesota Historical Society.)

Plymouth's Catholic community was first organized in 1856. Originally known as St. Francis Church, early members congregated in a tiny log chapel on the shore of Medicine Lake. Just 24 by 32 feet, this structure was replaced in 1876 by a wood-frame building measuring 36 by 80 feet. When the steeple bell was dedicated on November 5, 1876, the name was changed to St. Joseph's Church.

Mt. Olivet Church's roots are as the German Evangelical Lutheran Church, meeting at the Sandhoff home in the 1850s. Records were kept in German, and the Fitzer and Schmidt families were early members. In 1880, Mt. Olivet Chapel was constructed. Walls painted with the phrase "Godd mit uns" showcased the congregation's German heritage. A new structure was built in 1966, though Christmas Eve and Easter services are still held at the chapel.

This photograph shows Messiah Methodist Church in 1936. It is among the many structures housing the congregation throughout Plymouth's history. A Methodist society was first organized in the area in 1868, with its first log chapel constructed near Parkers Lake in 1871. The church was destroyed in a fire and rebuilt in 1889, featuring Peter Winnen's hand-carved altar. The church's present building opened in 1965, experiencing renovations throughout the decades.

It is believed that this photograph shows the altar Peter Winnen carved for Parkers Lake Methodist Church. The altar was partially destroyed by a fire. The sheaves of wheat are typical of Winnen's designs, along with naturalistic carved images of deer, leaves, flowers, and birds. Winnen taught wood carving to his daughters, who then shared the skill with the next generation.

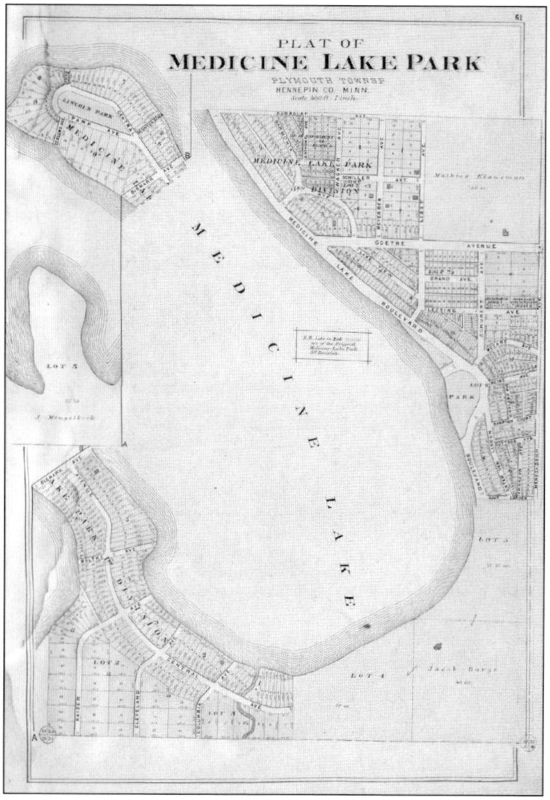

Soon, those outside of Plymouth began to take note of its beautiful lakes, charming landscapes, and convenient location. In the late 1880s, Minneapolis businessman and real estate developer Jacob Barge purchased over 450 acres around Medicine Lake, including over three miles of shoreline. He platted subdivisions of over 600 lots and began his sales pitch for the possibilities of life along the lake. The next step in his scheme was to incorporate a town to support his development plans. Despite an attempted court injunction by several Plymouth residents and farmers, Barge pushed through a ballot initiative, and the new town of Minneapolis Park was incorporated in 1891. In an interesting twist—and no doubt to Barge's dismay—the town only lasted two years.

Adeline Krienke Fitzer was born in Germany in 1872. She came to the United States as a young woman and married John Fitzer. This photograph shows the Fitzer farmhouse, near what is now Dallas Lane, just off of Fernbrook Lane. Pictured left to right are Karl, Bill, Marie, John, Lottie, Adeline, and Albert. Adeline's daughter Lottie married Ellsworth Turner, and they ran Turner's Store in Plymouth for many years.

James and Mary Smith Ryan's farmhouse is shown here around 1880. James and Mary were both born in Ireland and married in 1855. The couple had 12 children. A hand-colored photograph of the Ryan farm from 1914 shows a windmill and two impressive barns behind the house. Today, an interchange for Interstate 494 exists in its place.

In 1884, an important vote transpired at Dan Parker's house. Those voting "yes" stood at the west side of the house, outnumbering those standing to the east. Decision made: a town hall would be built. Thomas Ditter and Clemens Mengelkoch designed the structure in the Mengelkoch's kitchen, with Thomas responsible for lathing and plastering and Clem for carpentry. It was completed in 1885 for a cost of $503.

This stone bridge spanned Plymouth Creek on Fernbrook Lane, or "Town Hall Road." It was built in 1894 for a total cost of about $350. Town records show that Henry Mengelkoch was the stonemason on the project, for which he was paid $121.50. This photograph of the bridge shows Helen Mengelkoch and was taken in 1916 or 1917.

During this era, more and more people pursued outdoor recreation in response to the increasing industrialization of American cities. In the case of Minneapolis, many were drawn to the recreational opportunities provided by Plymouth area lakes, as seen in these two photographs taken in 1894 at Medicine Lake. In the photograph above, the formally attired staff of the *Saturday Spectator* spent a leisurely afternoon at the lake. The *Spectator* was a Minneapolis newspaper published weekly from 1879 to 1895. In the photograph below, members of the Laurel Social Club hosted a "Tally Ho" party, with their wagon full of party-goers and good cheer. (Above, courtesy of the Medicine Lake History Collection; below, courtesy of the Minnesota Historical Society.)

In 1883, the Soo Line Railroad was incorporated by several prominent businessmen with the purpose of providing an efficient way of transporting wheat to flour mills in Minneapolis. On December 6, 1886, a Soo Line station opened in Hamel, serving many Plymouth farmers. This c. 1895 photograph captures the arrival of harvesting machinery by a Soo Line train. (Courtesy of the Minnesota Historical Society.)

Before wheat could be transported to Minneapolis mills, there was the formidable task of harvesting it. Threshing was a team effort with large threshing crews working long days. This photograph shows a threshing crew on the Joseph Merz farm near County Road 24. The thresher's engine was fired with straw. Extra wagons followed the machine, gathering grain and carrying water for steam. (Courtesy of the West Hennepin County Pioneer Museum.)

Three

Life at the Turn of the Century 1900–1920

Located just 12 miles from downtown Minneapolis, Plymouth was a vital source of local food. Driving wagon loads of vegetables and fruit to Minneapolis markets was a routine aspect of a farmer's week. Tedious and tiring, this "commute" was changed forever by the advent of the Model T. This affordable, reliable automobile was embraced by many of Plymouth's farmers. Seemingly overnight, the distance between Plymouth and Minneapolis closed forever.

The automobile, along with the newly built Luce Electric Line, also changed the way Minneapolis residents looked at Plymouth. Plymouth, with its beautiful lakes, had long been a destination spot for picnickers, bathers, and anglers from the city. In the late 19th century, city dwellers began to purchase summer homes along Plymouth's lakeshores. By 1920, many of those summer homes were converted to year-round housing, their residents commuting to Minneapolis each morning and back to Plymouth each night.

Plymouth's commuter population did not see significant growth until decades later. Small pockets of prewar housing did develop around the west sides of Medicine Lake and Parkers Lake, the north end of Gleason Lake, and the intersection of Highway 55 and Old County Road 15. However, before any additional housing could be built, the town needed to develop its infrastructure. This came at a cost. The construction of roads, sewers, industrial areas, and shopping centers effectively displaced the majority of Plymouth's farmers.

These controversial changes, outlined explicitly in the *Plymouth Voter*, an independent newspaper of the 1950s–1970s, were far from the thoughts of Plymouth residents at the turn of the century. Back then, Plymouth, like every American town, faced a series of social, political, and cultural changes. This chapter focuses on those changes, which ranged from the mundane—jazz music, tight skirts, and bathing suits—to the national and international challenges of Prohibition, suffrage, and World War I.

Charles Trittelwitz is pictured above with his horses in front of his farmhouse around 1920. The house, built in either 1904 or 1910, included a basement for storing potatoes, cabbages, shelves of sauerkraut, and dill pickles. It did not have an indoor bathroom or running water until 1945. Prior to that, his wife, Edna Sandhoff Trittelwitz, pumped water from an outdoor cistern for washing purposes. The c. 1915 photograph below shows Louis Trittelwitz with a single bottom plow pulled by a three-horse team. The Trittelwitz farmhouse has been renovated and still stands on Kimberley Lane today, surrounded by a neighborhood of modern homes.

In 1913, rail was laid between Minneapolis and Parkers Lake as part of the Luce Electric Line. Sometimes referenced as an early 20th-century version of a light-rail corridor, the Luce Line provided passenger transport to many destination spots in existing communities surrounding Minneapolis. A popular stop in Plymouth was the Parkers Lake Dance Hall. (Courtesy of the Hennepin County Library.)

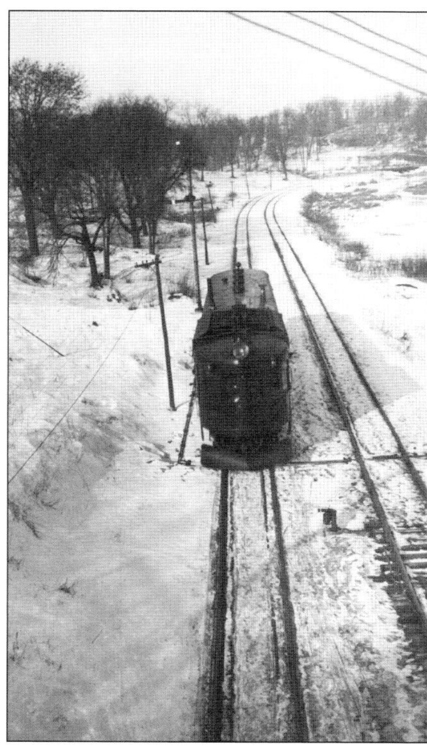

The Luce Line stop at Parkers Lake enhanced the lake's appeal for visitors from Minneapolis. Many businesses, clubs, and organizations from the city began hosting large picnics and gatherings at the lake. Developers took notice and began to capitalize on Plymouth's quiescent appeal, touting the short commute, open spaces, and recreational opportunities—a refrain still heard today. (Courtesy of the Minnesota Streetcar Museum.)

The Luce Line's ability to connect Plymouth to Minneapolis spurred real estate developers to capitalize on its potential as a charming suburb for those hoping to escape the bustle of the city. Two early subdivisions, Glen Grove and Sunset Acres, promised picturesque lake views, plenty of space for children to play, increasing property values, and short commutes to the city. Sunset Acres lots sold for $350.

The Luce Line had multiple stops along Medicine Lake, including Elmhurst Junction, located just 100 feet west of where West Medicine Lake Drive runs today. A 1915 report describes the stop as a 10-by-23-foot shed. It no doubt spurred the development of the Elmhurst neighborhood at Medicine Lake, platted in May 1912.

One prominent business that hosted its annual picnic at Parkers Lake was the Pillsbury Company. Picnic-goers were treated to games, athletic contests, and music. Another group that celebrated at the lake during this era was the Old-Timers Club of North Minneapolis. A 1920 advertisement for this event promised a square dance revival free of the more-trendy jazz music of the day. (Courtesy of the Minnesota Historical Society.)

Picnickers no doubt enjoyed activities on the water. An article advertising the YMCA Aquatic Tournament and Game Festival on May 12, 1917, suggested that "bathing suits are to be the height of fashion at Parkers Lake." Mabel Parker Brown, ancestor of Plymouth's original Parker family, is pictured here on the right in this undated photograph.

A canoe craze hit Minneapolis in the early 1900s, and area lakes were teeming with canoers. One historian compared it to the rollerblading fad of the 1990s. The canoeing trend was not without controversy, however, as debate arose over proper beach and boating attire for women. In 1914, F.C. Berry of the Minneapolis Park Board warned that the narrow skirts in fashion at the time were death traps for anyone attempting to swim if a canoe capsized. Similarly, the *Minneapolis Morning Tribune* ran an article with the headline "Girl Canoeists' Tight Skirts Menace Society." At the same time, women were not allowed to wear bathing suits more than four inches above the knee. Nevertheless, Mabel Parker Brown (right) and her friend, believed to be Orpha Moe, clearly did not let the issue stop them from hopping into a canoe on Parkers Lake.

The X.Y. Benefit Association Picnic was an annual Parkers Lake event sponsored by Wyman, Partridge & Company, a prominent dry goods company from Minneapolis. The program for the 1919 picnic included sack races, ball-throwing contests, tug-of-war, dancing, and a community sing. Rowboats could be rented for 25¢ and a towel and locker for 15¢.

Parkers Lake on the Luce Electric Lines

Thanks to its prime location along the Luce Line, the Joy Club, built in 1915 on the southeastern side of Parkers Lake, was a popular destination for summer events and weekend getaways. Its heyday was brief, however, as the Joy Club was destroyed in a fire in the late 1920s.

Bass Lake was another popular outpost for Minneapolitans capitalizing on Plymouth's liminality between country and city. This 1892 photograph captures the Minneapolis Gardener's Club gathering at Bass Lake. The popularity of garden clubs increased rapidly in the early 20th century, with members focusing both on private gardens and the cultivation of public spaces. (Courtesy of the Minnesota Historical Society.)

This group photograph captures attendees of the Danish Brotherhood in America picnic at Bass Lake on August 19, 1928. The Danish Brotherhood originally organized to support Danish immigrants; however, with tighter immigration policies in the 1920s, the DBA shifted to a focus on celebrating Danish heritage through social activities for families. One cannot help but note the commitment to ties and jackets for a picnic in August! (Courtesy of the Minnesota Historical Society.)

Albert Leroy Libby and his family took full advantage of the business and recreation opportunities made possible by Bass Lake. They owned a grocery and bottle shop on Bass Lake Road. Minutes from a 1908 Minneapolis City Council meeting show Albert's son George's application for a license to sell milk in the area. They also owned Libby's Pavilion, a dance hall that hosted several events throughout the year.

A boy is shown near the Libbys' Bass Lake House proudly displaying an impressive catch. An article published in the *Minneapolis Tribune* on January 1, 1914, reported that a small island on Bass Lake in Plymouth was the last parcel of land in Hennepin County claimed under the Homestead Act of 1862.

Plymouth lore credits Antoine LeCounte with the naming of Bass Lake. A fish survey taken in 2012 indicated that largemouth bass is still the dominant game fish in the lake. In this undated photograph, Albert Libby and his wife, Minnie, enjoy a day out on Bass Lake in their boat, named *You La You!*

Another important industry provided by Bass Lake was ice harvesting. Used to preserve food before refrigeration was widely available, ice was a valuable cold-weather "crop." Until the 1920s, horse-drawn plows cut grids across the lake's surface, and workers used five-foot hand saws to separate 22-inch-square blocks. Each block weighed between 250 and 300 pounds. This 1914 photograph captures a stack of ice ready for transport to a nearby icehouse. (Courtesy of the Minnesota Historical Society.)

Later, horses were replaced with gasoline-powered circular blades. The ice was stored in buildings insulated with hay and sawdust. Well-maintained ice houses preserved ice for an entire year. The harvest began in January and continued all day and through the night with moonlight and lanterns guiding the workers. It was not for those afraid of the Minnesota cold. The c. 1914 photograph above captures the ice harvest at Bass Lake by the People's Ice Company. The photograph below shows an extensive ice harvesting operation also on Bass Lake in Plymouth. (Both, courtesy of the Minnesota Historical Society.)

Originally from Sweden, John Engman first settled in Michigan with his wife, Johanna. He was injured in a copper mine explosion, and the couple decided to move to Minneapolis in 1885. John worked as a stonemason and Johanna was a licensed midwife, receiving training at the University of Minnesota. The Engmans longed for the rural life, so in 1898 they purchased the land at what is today the corner of Nathan Lane and East Medicine Lake Boulevard. With the help of their sons Eric, Albert, David, and Walfred, they started a resort business complete with picnic grounds and 35 rental boats. In the winter, they harvested ice from Medicine Lake and sold it to local businesses. Della and David Engman are shown standing in the photograph below.

In 1913, Johanna Engman died, and three of her sons continued operation of her resort on Medicine Lake. Around 1935, part of the Engmans' building was renovated to become Medicine Inn. This photograph shows how it looked in 1965. A business card lists beer on tap, ice cream, soft drinks, boat rentals, and a playground as reasons to stop by the inn. David Engman, pictured here with his horse and buggy, ran the business with his brothers until 1950. In 1967, the property was sold, and the buildings were razed for construction of the At-The-Lake Apartments.

This 1909 photograph shows the farmhouse of Joseph and Maria Ernst. Joseph arrived in New York in 1851. When a friend wagered his Minnesota farm in a card game, Joseph became interested in Minnesota, purchasing 80 acres in Plymouth in 1864. The friend's farm was next door, and Joseph purchased this land, too. It was inherited by Anna Ernst Mengelkoch, pictured here with husband Henry, daughter Laura (left), and niece Agnes.

On May 16, 1899, Catherine Milbert married Joseph and Maria Ernst's son, Anthony, and they began their lives together on Anthony's Plymouth farm. Catherine was an ardent supporter of education and was among the first female school board members in Minnesota. Upon her death, her son Walter created a family trust to support her descendants in their educational endeavors.

Anthony Ernst, shown here in this photograph from the late 1890s, was a trustee at St. Joseph's Community Parish. By 1906, the Ernsts had three children, six-year-old Mabel and her younger brothers, Richard and Irven. Concerned that the long walk to the District 95 schoolhouse would be too difficult for Mabel, the Ernsts sent her to live with relatives in Kansas City to attend school there. In December of that year, Anthony traveled by rail to Kansas City so Mabel could join her family for Christmas. Unfortunately, Mabel took ill and died on Christmas Eve. Catherine and Anthony eventually had eight children. Mabel and Irven are shown in the photograph to the right. (Right, courtesy of Genevieve Ernst Lane.)

This photograph shows Mathias, son of John Jordan, and his wife, Anna, in front of their Plymouth farmhouse in 1916. The Jordans had nine sons and two daughters. An aerial photograph taken during the late 1970s or early 1980s captures the Jordan farm, including this farmhouse.

One cannot help but wonder whether Mathias and Anna Jordan could have predicted in 1916 how their farm might grow and change over the decades. From Mathias's horse-drawn plow to the multiple vehicles parked in front of the farm's multiple outbuildings, the changes brought by time and technology are captured in the contrast of these images.

The Country Place Era of the late 19th and early 20th century took form beyond the edges of Minneapolis in gentleman farms that dotted Lake Minnetonka and extended into the Plymouth area. Gentlemen farmers showcased affluence in aesthetics over utility as they constructed elaborate barns, assembled premier show herds, and challenged the concept of the traditional family farm. Perhaps the best known of these farms in Plymouth was Freedom Farm, owned by milling magnate Fred G. Atkinson. Atkinson purchased his farm in the late 1920s, naming it after the "Freedom Flour" made in his mills. The farm, located north of Wayzata, was known for its show herd of Jersey cows. Atkinson imported a prize-winning bull called Lord of Les Jardins from the Isle of Jersey and accumulated over 150 purebred Jerseys. The best of Atkinson's herd competed in national competitions.

Freedom Farm remained in the dairy business through the 1930s. Milk was pasteurized and delivered around the Lake Minnetonka and Minneapolis areas, later taking on the name "Jersey Creamline." Atkinson died in 1940, and the prize-winning herd was auctioned. The land and buildings were sold and transitioned into a turkey farm.

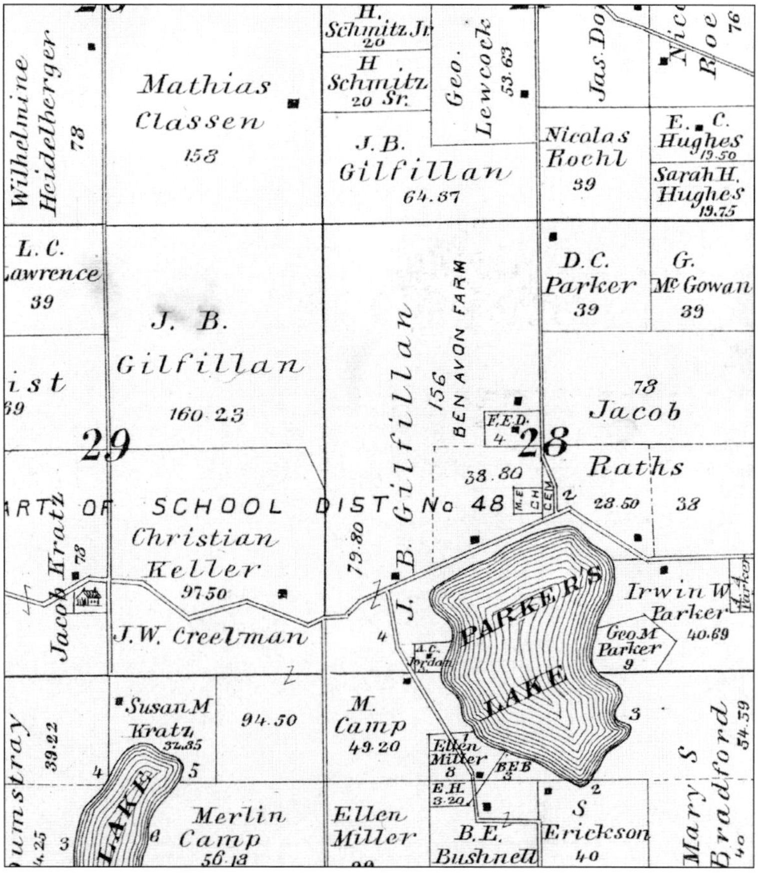

This 1898 map of Plymouth shows a large area of land as belonging to J.B. Gilfillan. John Gilfillan was a Minneapolis lawyer and politician who served as the Hennepin County Attorney, a University of Minnesota Regent, and a member of Congress for one term. Gilfillan wanted a summer home outside of the city and purchased approximately 500 acres for this purpose.

Known as "Ben Avon Farm," Gilfillan's summer home was far from the typical farmhouse peppering the Plymouth landscape. His Victorian-style country home had three floors with multiple fireplaces and bathrooms, French-tiled walls, a power generator, servants' quarters, and a grape arbor. Gilfillan also had a log cabin constructed for his children in 1900. Known as Deer Park, a replica of the cabin exists on the north shore of Parkers Lake.

The Gilfillan farm was sold to Earle Brown in the early 1920s and Gilfillan's blue-ribbon herd was sold at auction. In 1923, Brown sold the property to the city of Minneapolis to build a workhouse. Workhouse superintendent Arthur Birong is shown here with his children Jeanne and Jack around 1926.

Souvenir

School Dist. No. 48

Plymouth Twp.,

Hennepin County, Minn.

1902–1903

...PRESENTED BY...

AMELIA WESTBURG, Teacher

SCHOOL BOARD

Mr. A. Frick Mr. A. Johnson

Mr. A. Kreatz

D. C. Mackenzie, County Superintendent

The inside of this District 48 graduation program from 1903 lists 22 graduates. The previous year, District 48 and District 95 combined to celebrate the first group of eighth-grade graduates in Plymouth history, according to a *Minneapolis Morning Tribune* article. This ceremony was an evening celebration at the Parkers Lake schoolhouse that included recitations and musical performances. Pictured below in his baseball uniform is Allen Parker. Allen, along with Mabel, Harriet, Anna, and Lillian Parker, were among the 22 graduates listed in the graduation program. Also listed are members of the Frick, Heidelberger, Kreatz, and Anderson families.

Several tiny school districts existed in and around Plymouth throughout its early decades, including Districts 20, 23, 27, 47, 48, 51, 95, 104, 120, 123, and 127. District 104's building was called Oak Wood School and was located near where Station 73 Park & Ride is today along Highway 55. Later, Oak Wood became part of Wayzata Public Schools. The district opened a new building named Oakwood Elementary School in 1958.

This photograph shows the District 47 class of 1922 or 1923. The school was built in 1880 and located near Hamel on what is today the northeast corner of Rockford Road and Holly Lane. By the 1930s, Minnesota had over 3,000 school districts, and many of them were one-room schoolhouses such as this. One by one, Plymouth's old schoolhouses were destroyed. District 47 was burned by the Plymouth Fire Department in a 1973 training exercise.

This District 95 class picture was taken sometime between 1916 and 1918. The boy in the front row with the white cap is Walter Ernst, and the tall boy in the back row is Frank McGowan. Anyone who has ever attempted to take a photograph of a large group of children will no doubt appreciate the two stocking-capped boys at the right who failed to look at the camera.

This portrait showcases District 95's eighth-grade graduating class with neatly rolled diplomas from the era. The front row includes Roland Schiebe, Anna Cavanagh, and Walter Ernst, among others. The back row includes Irven Ernst and Raymond Mengelkoch. The photograph was taken at C.H. Galbraith Studio in Minneapolis.

William Cavanagh, standing in the back row with the tie and vest, was given a farm as a wedding gift when he married Mary McGowan in 1889. This photograph was taken by a traveling photographer in front of their farmhouse in June 1901. It is believed several people in the photograph are from the neighboring Donahue family.

On October 3, 1914, friends and relatives of William and Mary Cavanagh threw them an elaborate, weekend-long party for their 25th wedding anniversary. Guests came by wagon or the Luce Line and danced all night until the early hours of the morning, when they enjoyed breakfast served by the couple's 12 children and a game of hide-and-seek. The couple was gifted with a three-piece parlor set that cost $125.

William and Mary's son William Jr. married Marie Francis Cain on October 12, 1927, on the kind of Minnesota autumn day when four inches of snow already blanketed the ground. William served in the US Army, started Cavanagh Brothers Builders with several family members, and was highly involved in the community, including serving as a school board member. The Cavanagh School (now closed) in Crystal was named for William in 1958.

This photograph captures the wedding day of Anna Cavanagh, daughter of William and Mary Cavanagh, and Raymond Mengelkoch. Many of Anna's colorful memories vivify Cavanagh family stories. One such story is how her grandfather Patrick was able to pay cash for the 80 acres he bought near Parkers Lake in 1856. Anna playfully suggested it might have been acquired thanks to the wine cellar under her grandfather's front porch.

As the new century unfolded, the compelling emergence of the automobile transformed daily life in Plymouth. This transition is captured in the contrast of these two photographs. In the image above, taken in 1915, Henry Schiebe courts Mary Dressel in a horse-drawn buggy. The Dressel farm was located in the Ridgedale area of Minnetonka. One has to wonder if Mary was impressed by the rather stately horse. In the photograph below, Carl Eckstrom in shown ice fishing with his 1915 Model T on Medicine Lake. While the model of car has changed across the century, the sight of vehicles scattered across Medicine Lake during ice fishing season is still familiar. If only Eckstrom had social media to share his successful catch.

Henry Bertrand was born in Copenhagen in 1865 and grew up on a farm overlooking the North Sea. At the age of 29, he traveled to Canada, where he earned degrees in chemistry and pharmacy. He married Hilda in 1895 and moved to Minneapolis. Henry applied his knowledge of chemistry to developing food and household products, including pancake mix, apple cider vinegar, and laundry detergent. Missing the waterfront view of his childhood, he purchased land at Medicine Lake to build a new summer house. Completed in 1910, the two-story home included an upstairs sun porch and a tuck-under garage for Henry's Buick. Soon, Henry and his sons, pictured below, began to appreciate the advantages of suburban life and started commuting to Minneapolis from Medicine Lake throughout the winter as well—an audacious venture considering the quality of roads at the time.

Henry and Hilda had four sons, Henry George, Victor, Robert, and William, and two daughters, Josephine and Nell. The entire family contributed to the family business, mixing, bottling, billing, or delivering products across Minneapolis. In their free time, they took advantage of the recreational opportunities available to those living on Medicine Lake, as evident in these 1917 photographs. The Bertrand business, along with life on the lake, was generational. In 1922, Victor invited Marie Kort to a family outing at the lake. She loved it as much as the family did. After they married in 1927, Victor had a house built on West Medicine Lake Drive, not too far from the original family home.

Eventually, the Bertrand business began to focus on their most successful product: dill pickles. In the pre-refrigeration days, pickles were especially popular, and the Bertrands soon had a factory that mechanized every step of the process with one exception: pickle packing. It turned out only human hands could complete this step to perfection. (Courtesy of Debra Bertrand Palmquist.)

The brine-soaked pickles were fermented in large oak barrels fastened tight with hoops by a cooper and were moved using a large elevator. The factory could turn out 10,000 jars of product a day, and the Bertrand line of products were shipped for distribution as far away as the Pacific coast. (Courtesy of Debra Bertrand Palmquist.)

As the United States entered World War I on April 6, 1917, Pres. Woodrow Wilson called upon those on the home front to apply their energies towards the support of the Red Cross. Volunteers across Minnesota joined in this effort operating canteens at railroad depots, collecting food and comfort items, supporting soldiers' families, and organizing events at Fort Snelling. These photographs show Plymouth's Red Cross volunteers from Parkers Lake (above) and Bass Lake. By the time the war ended in November 1918, the Red Cross had established itself as an essential humanitarian organization.

A search of Plymouth in Twin Cities' newspapers in the early 20th century reveals an extensive collection of articles concerning applications "to sell intoxicating liquors." These often mention Bass Lake House or the Farmer's Home Hotel. Several articles detail a 1904 denial of a Bass Lake liquor license due to the saloon's proximity to a schoolhouse. A *Minneapolis Journal* article from August 15, 1904, details a 35-to-19 vote in Plymouth to move the schoolhouse, thus allowing for the saloon license that previously had been "too near the temple of learning." The decision was met with strong opposition. In this same era, the Women's Christian Temperance Union's Minnesota branch was busy promoting the benefits of Prohibition. This photograph shows Minnesota women dressed in white advocating for this cause. (Courtesy of the Minnesota Historical Society.)

There are some interesting stories behind the architecture of several Plymouth homes during this era. One example is the William "Willie" Hughes house, pictured above, that today faces Highway 101. The original Hughes' family farmhouse burned down in 1914, and a new catalog kit house was ordered to replace it. Most likely, it was a Sears Catalog home known as a "4-Square" or "Corn Belt Cube" house, one of nearly 70,000 house kits sold by Sears between 1908 and 1940. Usually delivered by train and then hauled to the farm by horse and wagon, these kit homes had over 370 variations and allowed the buyer to select such features as light fixtures, woodwork, and cabinets. Another interesting home is this converted Pullman Car house built around 1928. It was located on what is today called Magnolia Lane.

The photograph above shows the blacktopping of a Plymouth road in the late 1930s. Town records from the 1930s show that frequent expenditures for the community included dragging roads, setting up snow fences, and catching gophers. There were also frequent disbursements of funds to provide food, clothing, or rent money for those in need. Herb's Corner stands in the background. Built in 1933 by Herb Johnson, Herb's Corner was a gas station servicing southwest Plymouth. In the aerial photograph below, taken between 1934 and 1936, Herb's Corner stands alone at the center, surrounded by a wide expanse of farmland. By the 1970s, this farmland had been converted to shops and restaurants, with Herb's Corner situated at the busy intersection of County Road 6 and 101.

Four

Building a Legacy 1920–1950

It is easy to imagine early-20th-century Plymouth as an idyllic American farming community, far removed from the troubles of the world. However, its residents have long known that some troubles are impossible to escape. Since its inception, Plymouth chose to engage with, not hide from, the nation's collective struggles. From the Civil War to World War II, Plymouth's residents have volunteered their lives to serve on distant battlefields.

When crime, poverty, and substance abuse threatened the future of a generation besieged by the Great Depression, the battlefield was brought to Plymouth. However reluctant the town may have been initially, it played a significant role in the country's rehabilitation. Between 1927 and 1931, two institutions—the Minneapolis Workhouse and Mission Farms—were built to help the desperate and the destitute transform their lives.

Mission Farms' founder, Rev. William Paul, believed in the dignity and worth of those most in need. Beginning in 1927, he helped them find that worth by providing food, shelter, and meaningful work on the farm. By 1933, Mission Farms had gained a national reputation. Government officials serving under Franklin D. Roosevelt visited Mission Farms to study its success. Mission Farms became the model for Depression-era transient camps, which were designed to offer migrant workers a place to rest, eat, and regain their self-respect. The Civilian Conservation Camps also followed the Mission Farms model, providing young, unskilled, and unemployed men the opportunity for meaningful work and education.

Though the farms no longer exist, Mission Farms and the Minneapolis Workhouse remain an important presence in Plymouth as Missions Inc. and the Hennepin County Adult Corrections Facility. These institutions see thousands of individuals through some of the most difficult periods in their lives. At any given time, 477 inmates at the adult corrections facility learn transferable job skills, attend classes, and receive mental health and chemical dependency assistance, if needed. Approximately 3,600 people experiencing chemical addition, homelessness, and violence turn to Missions Inc. each year for its renowned treatment center, long-term care facility, and shelter from domestic violence.

This chapter focuses on the legacy Plymouth began to build in the first half of the 20th century. The fortitude and determination demonstrated by the townsfolk during the Great Depression and World War II carried through into the 1950s as Plymouth saw its greatest transformation yet.

An unidentified member of the Mengelkoch family poses next to a steam-powered tractor in the photograph to the left. Steam-powered tractors were replaced by faster-starting internal combustion models after World War I. The affordability of the gas-powered tractor in the 1920s allowed farmers to shift away from horse-drawn equipment. Henry Schiebe's 1923 Fordson tractor shown in the photograph below was a popular choice during this evolution. These four-cylinder tractors were manufactured in the United States from 1917 to 1928, with over 100,000 produced in 1923 alone.

Robert Blodgett began his dairy operation with just three cows but soon became known throughout the region for his innovation in the industry. Blodgett built this dairy barn in 1925 with a glass front so people could view the milking parlor inside, a first for the area. Advertised as Blodgett-Guernsey Dairy, milk was delivered throughout the Minneapolis area for just 13¢ per quart. The barn, located just north of Wayzata on Highway 101, was destroyed by a fire in 1937. The business was sold to Ohleen Dairy of Minneapolis, and the land was subdivided for homes and an electrical substation was constructed. Ohleen Dairy was known for its interesting marketing strategies, including a downtown Minneapolis billboard featuring a giant diapered toddler named "Diaper Dan" and the slogan "Time for a Change." (Both, courtesy of the Wayzata Historical Society.)

Founded in 1895, Union City Mission began as a partnership between Minneapolis churches and business leaders with the mission to help the city's homeless and unemployed populations. In 1927, it was expanded to include a working farm called Mission Farms. Located along the north shore of Medicine Lake, the farm's residency peaked during the Great Depression. With over 93 acres of woodland and 8,000 feet of shoreline, Mission Farms' idyllic landscapes provided opportunities for off-season and unemployed workers to develop skills, as buildings, and lives, were reimagined. Perhaps the best example is the Tabernacle, built from the bricks of the National Hotel, known for its decadent Dutch Room restaurant and Prohibition raids. By the end of the Depression, over 1,000 Mission Farms workers had acquired self-supporting work.

The inside of the Tabernacle captured Mission Farms' pragmatic commitment to transformation. If chairs, tables, and in this case, pews, were needed, they could be constructed from the surrounding trees. If farm equipment was needed, it could be patched together at the onsite blacksmith and machine shop. Even mattresses were rebuilt on-site as befitting of both the Depression-era zeitgeist and the organization's mission.

The Tabernacle's windows were a gift from a Plymouth church, and it is believed the columns supporting the roof were trees logged on site. In fact, a postcard from the era claims the columns sprouted leaves the first year. At capacity, the space could seat 1,200 people.

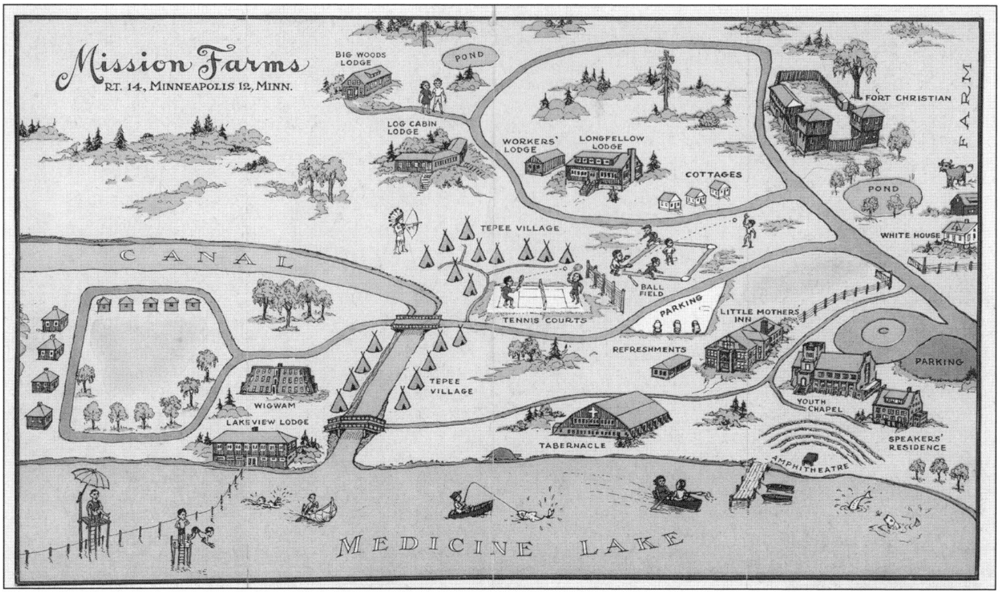

Mission Farms workers returned to fields, forests, and mines during the summer months. That void was soon filled by camps, conferences, and conventions. Mission Farms became the perfect setting for groups wishing to connect their faith or purpose to the possibilities of Minnesota summers. Soon, even more structures dotted the scene, as evident in this brochure.

The Speaker's Residence, also known as Wallace Lodge, stood next to the Chapel. A 1937 church newsletter encouraged youth to consider attending camp at Mission Farms, emphasizing recreation, fellowship, and the opportunity "to become better acquainted with God and His outdoors." The same newsletter states a cost of $4 for a five-day stay and encourages attendees to pack a bathing suit, Bible, and a "cheery disposition."

This interior view of the Chapel showcases the contrast between stately and rugged, with elegant windows and a dramatically sloped roof rising over rough-hewn pews. On-site timber was also used to construct an outdoor amphitheater, shown below. It has been said that between 1929 and the late 1960s, nearly a million people visited the camp from all parts of the country. Well-known religious leaders came to the camp, including Billy Graham, who held service there. Music was elemental to camp services. *The Campers Hymnal: Songs for the Out-of-Doors*, published in 1941, is one such guidebook for those voices joined in worship midst the bucolic surroundings.

Campers at Mission Farms had an interesting array of accommodations to choose from, including a wigwam, igloos, and a tepee village. The fascinating Wigwam Inn had three floors and an observation deck. The pod-style, heavily shingled igloos, of which there were at least six, likely required some imagination to evoke an icy chill during a Minnesota summer night.

Another interesting dormitory option for campers was Fort Christian, shown here. The structure was designed to replicate a Western-style fort with trim palisade walls. Most visual evidence of the camp's unique buildings is preserved through postcards from the era, with at least one known postcard showcasing the fort.

More than 30 tepees comprised the Indian Village and canal area at Mission Farms. Most tepees housed two campers, though some may have been modified to hold more. They included a canopied storm door and tidy framed windows, though inside accommodations are not visible. Evidence of the canal remains near the boat landing at French Regional Park. The inclusion of Fort Christian, Wigwam Inn, and the tepees at the camp reflects the romanticization of the western frontier that permeated this era. Though they no longer exist today, these structures illustrate the ongoing challenges surrounding the oversimplification and mischaracterization of Native culture.

The camp also included a replica of Abraham Lincoln's log cabin. Located near the tennis courts and the Indian Village, the cabin was designed with the exact size specifications of Lincoln's birthplace. Every detail was carefully considered—the cabin even included hand-hewn shingles. Only one known postcard view of the cabin exists.

Most parents who have sent a child to camp will not be surprised to learn that a common message sent on Mission Farms postcards was about the food. Apparently, the food received mixed reviews ranging from "Fantastic!" to "Send food, I'm starving!" This postcard shows the dining room at Little Mother's Inn with handmade tables spread with white tablecloths.

Among the varied recreational activities captured in images and messages on multiple postcards is swimming, both at the pool and in the lake. Very few existing images of the camp show people, but this one of the pools is clearly an exception. Other activities included boating and playing tennis on clay courts.

The Bath House Pavilion was later converted to lodging and renamed the Lakeview Lodge, shown here. It was located along the shore near what is now the swimming beach at French Regional Park. Other buildings used as dormitories included Smith Lodge, located near the main entry of the camp, and Longfellow Lodge, located near the road leading into the woods.

Methodist camp meetings were an annual summer tradition in Minnesota, beginning with the first in 1855. Providing attendees the opportunity for fellowship under the trees and a chance to hear preachers from all over the country, old-time camp meetings were held at Red Rock from 1868 until they were moved in Mission Farms in 1938. The photograph above from June 1940 shows campers engaged in a baseball game at the Red Rock Camp Meeting at Medicine Lake. The photograph to the left shows Dorothy Dilts inspecting the famous "red rock" on-site at Mission Farms as part of the Christian Youth Camp at Medicine Lake. (Both, courtesy of the Hennepin County Library.)

Much of the history and lore of Medicine Lake and Mission Farms is preserved through campy postcards. The back of this postcard, which could be mailed for just 1¢, advises the receiver on "How to Kiss Deliciously." Among the tips offered to gentlemen is one reminding not to smack one's lips "as you would after imbibing a Bacchanalian draught."

On October 5, 1948, Pioneer House, one of the first residential treatment centers for substance abuse in the area, opened on the Mission Farms property. Led by Pat Cronin, the first residents were housed at Little Mother's Inn. Pioneer House was known for a high recovery rate, and their work was documented by Yale researchers hoping to replicate this success.

In the early 1920s, the city of Minneapolis purchased the old J.B. Gilfillan estate from Earle Brown as the site for a new workhouse. The citizens of Plymouth did not welcome the Minneapolis Workhouse. A letter written on June 26, 1923, by town clerk Herb Johnson shares concerns about its existence so near a "thickly populated community." Johnson also pursued possible funding for an injunction effort. Eventually, the protest ran out of fuel, and the workhouse opened at Parkers Lake. The new workhouse was built in 1931. A *Tribune* article from 1924 estimated it would cost $1 million to build an administration building with four wings, each holding 99 cells. Plans also included guards' quarters, a dining room, kitchen, bakery, cement block factory, workshops, a women's dormitory, and a separate residence for the superintendent. (Above, courtesy of the Hennepin County Library; below, courtesy of the Minnesota Historical Society.)

Before finalizing the plans for the new Minneapolis Workhouse at Parkers Lake, Supt. Dr. Lockwood and another member of the Committee on Penal and Correctional Institutions visited workhouses in several eastern cities, including Sing Sing in New York. In his May 1923 report, Lockwood emphasized the importance of making the new workhouse a "correctional institution," as opposed to a "conventional jail." He also recommended separate cell blocks instead of dormitory-style facilities, a plan that was carried out as evidenced by the photograph at right. Several photographs of the workhouse from the early 20th century show prisoners engaged in work throughout the facility: making bricks, removing tree stumps, and working in the barbershop. The photograph below features an inmate feeding chickens on the farm. (Both, courtesy of the Hennepin County Library.)

Until 1931, inmates were transported daily to the workhouse's 486-acre farm. The "piggery" on-site was highly successful, and local farmers frequently stopped to inspect the operation. The workhouse's farming operations ceased in 1970, and in the late 1980s, a portion of the land was given to Plymouth for Parkers Lake Park. (Courtesy of the Hennepin County Library.)

The superintendent's residence was completed in 1933. Decades later, in the 1980s, it was torn down during the development of Parkers Lake Park, and a picnic pavilion took its place. Another image of the workhouse from this era shows a separate guards' quarters at the site. (Courtesy of the Hennepin County Library.)

During the 1930s, many events were held at Libby's on Bass Lake, including the 1939 Heidelberg Club Picnic. The purpose was to celebrate German culture and heritage. The event's speaker was former Wisconsin governor Philip LaFollette. A month later, Germany invaded Poland to start World War II, and the club faded.

Souvenir Program

of

The Old Heidelberg Club

PICNIC

Sunday, August 6th, 1939

LIBBY'S---BASS LAKE

MINNEAPOLIS

5 Miles Northwest of Robbinsdale on County Road 10

While the legend crediting a Minneapolis firefighter with inventing softball in 1895 has been debunked, what can be proven is that the game spread in popularity throughout the Minneapolis area. During the Great Depression, softball provided a welcome distraction. This 1939 photograph captures Plymouth's softball team. Genevieve Ernst Lane, third from left in the second row, reported that the team's uniforms were blue and gold wool gabardine, and they played area teams from Dayton and Brooklyn Park.

By the 1930s, growing enrollment in District 95 necessitated more classroom space. In 1939, the Cavanagh Brothers constructed a brick building next to the old one-room schoolhouse. To the great joy of the students, they officially moved into the new building over winter break, starting the school year in one building and ending it in another. The photograph below shows the new District 95 building just to the right of the 1872 one-room schoolhouse. The new building cost $30,000 and included two classrooms, a small auditorium, a kitchen, and indoor plumbing.

Throughout the 1940s, District 95 faced annual enrollment increases of 15 to 25 percent. This, along with the need for definitive junior high and high school programs, contributed to the decision in 1946 to consolidate with Wayzata Schools. From that point forward, the building was known as Beacon Heights School. After many additions and renovations over the decades, the school closed in 1982. Beacon Heights School took its name from the beacon light tower that guided airplanes to Wold–Chamberlain Field in Minneapolis. The beacon, which looked similar to the one at Indian Mounds Park in St. Paul (pictured right), was located on a hill near present-day Fire Station No. 1. (Below, courtesy of the Minnesota Historical Society.)

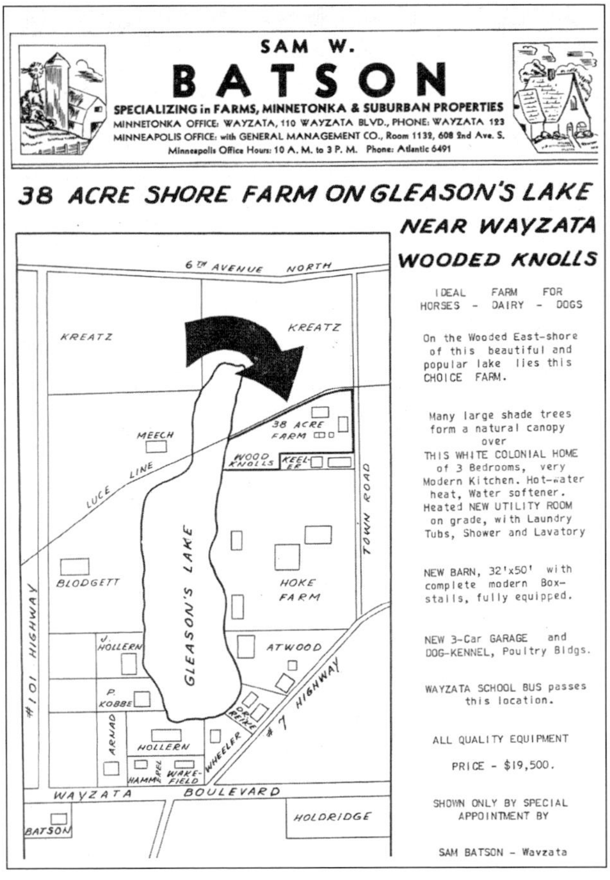

This 1940 picture shows the students of Medicine Lake School, also known as District 51. The teacher's name on the sign is "H. Higgins." One has to wonder why all of the students have their arms crossed, including the three boys in the second row who also linked their arms together.

This real estate flyer from 1945 shows the owners of the land around Gleason Lake, including Blodgett Dairy and John Hollern. Hollern was known for his herd of 40 Jerseys bred from stock at the Vanderbilt Biltmore Farms in North Carolina. Hollern donated 15 acres of his land to Wayzata Public Schools. The land was used for the administration building and Gleason Lake Elementary.

The Apple Blossom Inn at Medicine Lake was a nightclub owned by Charles Levissee. The Apple Blossom's advertisements touted an orchestra for dancing, a private dining room, aged steak, and space for bridge parties. According to an article published in *Billboard* magazine, the club was destroyed in a fire on August 12, 1946. The cause of the fire was the explosion of an oil storage tank in an adjacent barn. The loss was estimated at $15,000. The headline article of the same publication detailed outdoor music events being canceled due to the polio epidemic, including those at the Minnesota State Fair. (Courtesy of the Minnesota Historical Society.)

In 1899, the Minnesota state legislature passed a bill supporting traveling libraries. However, it was not until the early 1920s that the Hennepin County Public Library began bookmobile services. This photograph captures the bookmobile delivering books to a group of delighted children. Plymouth did not have its own free-standing library until 1995. (Courtesy of the West Hennepin County Pioneer Museum.)

In the 1940s, the Pretzel Inn was located at the southeast corner of Rockford Road and Fernbrook Lane. The business was run by Marie and Carl Link and was next door to the Turner's General Store, run by Ellsworth and Lottie Turner. The Turner and Link families are shown here in front of the Pretzel Inn.

Robert Ernst ran Ernst Grocery and Ice Cream Store during the 1920s. The store was located near the intersection of Highway 55 and Interstate 494. Pictured behind the store's shiny counter are Polly Ernst and Lorraine Begin. In the second photograph, a group of children is pictured outside of the Ernst store next to a sign for Franklin Ice Cream. Franklin Ice Cream was produced by the Franklin Cooperative Creamery in Minneapolis. Founded in 1919, in its heyday, the co-op produced nearly 80 percent of the Twin Cities' milk supply. The sign advertises the product as "purer because heathized."

The photograph to the left shows Harvey Schiebe in his World War II Army uniform standing with his wife Fern, his parents Mary and Henry, and his sons Lowell and Gary. In the photograph below, Harvey poses with his female relatives, who display a wide range of emotions regarding his imminent deployment. After the war, Harvey returned to Plymouth. Along with his brother Leon, he opened Schiebe's Hardware in 1955. The store was the cornerstone of the town's first strip mall for the next 40 years. Harvey was also a charter member of the Plymouth Fire Department and a founding member of the Plymouth Historical Society. He contributed many important artifacts to its collection, including his carefully preserved World War II and fireman's uniforms.

Andy Ahlstrom visited his brother Arvid and his sister-in-law Bertha at their home on Medicine Lake during a furlough from World War II. Andy joined the armed forces on March 11, 1942, serving with the 12th Army Air Force B-26 Marauders during the war. Before taking this leave, he had been in Casablanca, Malta, Sardinia, and Corsica. (Courtesy of the West Hennepin County Pioneer Museum.)

Louise Reary joined the Women's Army Corps in 1942. She was stationed at Hammer Field in Fresno, California, where she performed skilled clerical and administrative tasks in service to her country. After World War II, Louise and her husband, Clarence Parks, settled in Medicine Lake. Louise joined the nursing home staff at Mission Farms in 1968, working there for 42 years until retiring at the age of 90. (Courtesy of Becky Herke.)

By the 1940s, the economy of Plymouth was dominated by small-scale agriculture: truck farms with their typical 160 acres, 20 or so cows, dirt roads, and products sold fresh rather than processed before selling. With the population of the Twin Cities metropolitan area nearing 750,000, there was a large market for perishable goods such as vegetables, berries, milk, cream, and eggs. Land prices were reasonable, and this mode of agriculture resulted in a high income per acre. The photograph above shows Henry Schiebe with his cabbage harvest. The photograph to the left shows a child inspecting Hugo Broman's cabbages for sale at the Minneapolis Farmers Market in 1942. (Left, courtesy of the Hennepin County Library.)

By the 1950s, the Medicine Lake Bus Company was providing service from Medicine Lake, Plymouth, Golden Valley, and Maple Grove to downtown Minneapolis. A 1954 article from *Mass Transportation* magazine states that the orange and black buses carried over 200,000 riders a year. Many were shoppers headed to Dayton's, Donaldson's, or Powers in Minneapolis on what they affectionately nicknamed "the Rocket" line.

Medicine Lake Bus driver Edward Olson collects tickets from a cheerful-looking group in this photograph from September 1945. Pictured from left to right, passengers Joan Ostberg, Barbara Brimmer, Lynn Anderson, and Lois Nelson hand Olson their tickets as they board a bus headed from Minneapolis to Medicine Lake. (Courtesy of the Hennepin County Library.)

In 1941, Ukranian Day was held at Bass Lake Park. Pictured from left to right are Pastusnenko, Koshuba, Shai, and Jaseniuk, members of the Ukrainian Folk Ballet of the Twin Cities. The dance group entertained the audience with routines while donning the traditional costume of the Zaporozhian Cossacks. (Courtesy of the Hennepin County Library.)

At some point in the 1930s, Lonnie Flosseth decided to transport this house from the Medicine Lake peninsula across the frozen lake to a new location. The house featured a porch with large glazed windows. It must be noted that not a single window cracked when the home was moved. (Courtesy of the Minnesota Historical Society.)

Five

A City on the Rise
1950–Present

In the early 1950s, the square-shaped town of Plymouth saw its borders change. A group of townspeople, spearheaded by Les Johantgen, Charles Brudigan, and Ernest Ertl, voted to secede from Plymouth in 1944. Their new village, Medicine Lake, was situated entirely within Plymouth's borders on a small peninsula jutting into Medicine Lake. A few years later, the nearby city of Wayzata annexed the southwest corner of Plymouth's land.

Postwar suburban development threatened to carve additional slices from Plymouth. It was time for Plymouth to assert itself as a community. In Minnesota, an entire township can incorporate as a village or city. On May 10, 1955, a special election vote passed 747 votes to 163, making Plymouth a village. The first village election was held in June. Henry Sahly was voted the village's first mayor, and Phillip Eckes, Thomas Keefe, Allen Kreatz, and Karl Theis were elected as the village's first council.

From the beginning, village government was careful to create comprehensive, long-term plans to set Plymouth on the right course. Essentially beginning with a blank canvas, Plymouth had to design new roads, name its streets, develop zoning ordinances, create a sewer and water system, form police and fire departments, and craft a plan for parks and trails. Smart city planning led to successful, sustainable growth, unlike the first failed development in Plymouth back in 1857.

Today, Plymouth has completed the majority of the projects it developed in the 1950s, including building over 170 miles of trails, 1,700 acres of parks, and amenities such as the Hilde Performance Center, Plymouth Creek Center, Ice Center, and the innovative public-private partnership with Lifetime Fitness. This, combined with a strong business sector and first-class education programs, led *Money* magazine to name Plymouth the "Best Place to Live in the Nation" in 2008. This chapter focuses on how it got there.

A late 1950s council meeting held at the original town hall building is captured here. From left to right are Allan Kretz, Karl Theis, Mayor Howard Anderson, Herb Johnson, Henry Sahly, and an unidentified man. During this era, the Parks Commission, the Planning Commission, and the Building Code Commission were established.

The original 1885 town hall hosted council meetings until the early 1960s. During the Great Depression, the building served as a food pantry, providing bags of food to those in need, as well as providing a forum for boxing matches. One such fight between Frank Leur and Adrian Ernst resulted in a decisive victory for Ernst, who then drove his opponent home at the end of the bout.

The Zuhrah Shrine Horsemen purchased the Golden Valley Riding Academy in 1948. Located east of Parkers Lake where Fernbrook Lane intersects County Road 6, the acquisition included a barn, riding area, and a bunkhouse on 13 acres. The property was expanded to house about 40 horses by 1951. In 1955, the operation was moved to Bloomington, and the land was sold for a housing development. The Zuhrah Horsemen were well-known for intricate routines, best showcased in their annual "Show-deo." The Show-deo was held in Plymouth in 1949 and 1950 before moving to the Minnesota State Fairgrounds. A perfect example of Show-deo showmanship is captured in this photograph of Dinah, a horse who kneeled as the stadium lights dimmed. To add to the theatrical display, the "Horse Prayer" was read, Dinah was led off stage, the house lights were raised, and the audience was left wondering where Dinah might have gone. (Both, courtesy of the Zuhrah Shriners.)

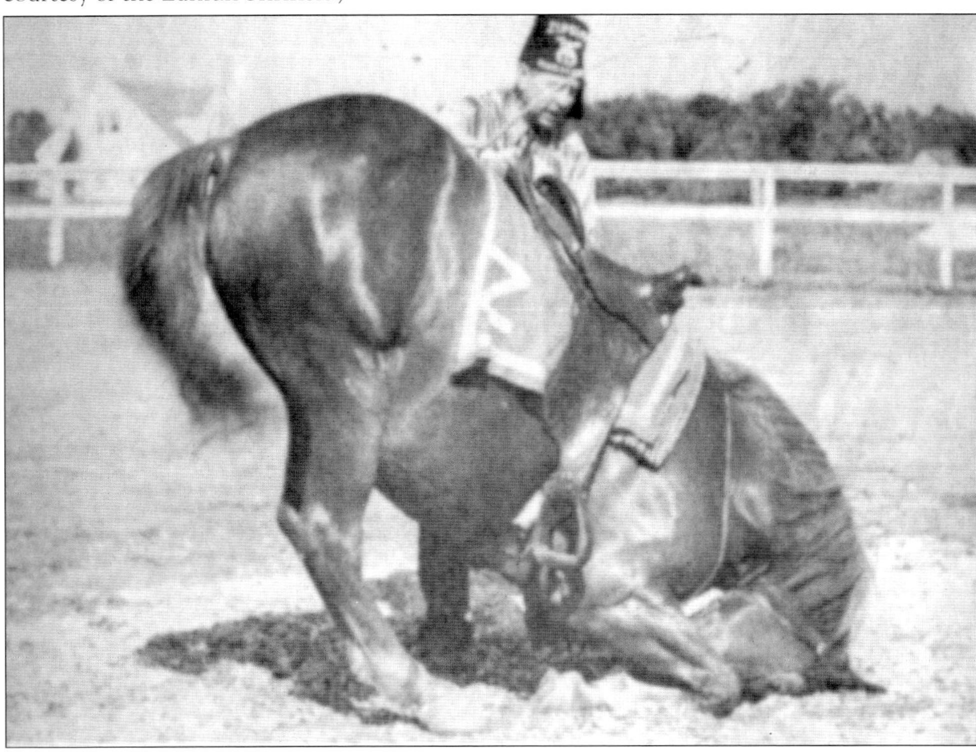

The Schiebe family built the Plymouth Shopping Center in the 1950s, seen above in this undated aerial photograph. Located at Highway 55 and Medicine Lake Road, many businesses came and went over the years. One that remained an anchor for decades was Schiebe's Hardware. Brothers Harvey and Leon Schiebe, pictured below, opened the store in 1955 and operated the business for over 40 years, finally closing in 1997. Advertisements for the store, as published in the *Plymouth Voter*, declared it "Your Store of Service." The shopping center was empty of tenants by 2006.

The Susie-Q was opened in 1957 by business partners Marvin Sieloff, Bill Sheets, and Ken Johnson. On any summer evening, one might have spotted carhops busily delivering the restaurant's most crowd-pleasing dish, half a chicken served with fries, toast, and cranberry sauce—all for just 99¢. The Susie-Q was a popular destination for families, date nights, and anyone who wanted a quick, tasty meal.

The Flying Tiger Bar opened in 1954. Prior to this, the building served as a blacksmith shop, a jail, a train station, the Jail House Inn, the Royal King Inn, and the Legion Club. The changes reflect Plymouth's growth over the decades. The Flying Tiger was destroyed in a fire in 1996.

Ivy Odegaard purchased her little country tavern, Ivy's Place, in 1960. Located on County Road 9 and Old Rockford Road, the tavern had a series of owners prior to Ivy and originally began as a gas station. The site's first liquor license was acquired in 1933, after the repeal of Prohibition. Ivy sold the property in the late 1980s. The building was burned to provide parking for Mt. Olivet Church.

Charlie's Store, located on the west side of Medicine Lake, is shown here in this 1966 photograph. Charlie's had several owners throughout the years, including the Krumholz, Schiebe, and Bowman families. The store sold bait and groceries and rented boats. Next door to Charlie's was Haley's Garage, pictured in the background.

Nat Day ran a garage and tow truck business on Medicine Lake. Day was a charter member of the Plymouth Volunteer Fire Department. He was also an Abraham Lincoln impersonator. Several photographs exist of Day dressed as Honest Abe for President's Day festivities, complete with Lincoln's signature beard, somber suit, and top hat.

This c. 1965 photograph shows Horstman's Dairy Bar. Horstman's was located on the west side of Medicine Lake. While all were welcome to shop at Horstman's, the store's one rule was well known among children: no touching the candy bars until they were paid for.

In 1950, a new Wayzata High School building was constructed on Vicksburg Lane. It opened in 1951 and served grades 7 through 12 until 1961. Today, the building is called West Middle School. What is today Central Middle School housed the high school from 1961 until 1997, when the current facility opened on Peony Lane. (Courtesy of the Hennepin County Library.)

Previously, high school classes were held in this 1922 building designed in the distinctive adobe Pueblo Revival style. Located in Wayzata with a view of Lake Minnetonka, the building was renamed Widsten School in 1953 in memory of principal Halvor Widsten. The school, beloved for its high ceilings, old-fashioned coat rooms, cozy fireplace, and overhead balconies in the gym, closed in 1989. (Courtesy of the Hennepin County Library.)

In 1956, Oakwood school, also known as District 104, consolidated with Wayzata Public Schools. Several other districts joined Wayzata at this time, and the district was renumbered as 284. A close viewing of this Oakwood School Class of 1953 photograph reveals the educational technology typical of the day: a portable phonograph, a set of carefully ordered encyclopedias, and an AM tabletop radio.

In April 1957, the Wayzata school board authorized a $1.1 million bond to build a new school and repair two other buildings. A site committee was formed. In October 1957, Wayzata Public Schools purchased 41.6 acres of land from the Kreatz family for $54,080. A new school building with a familiar name was constructed at this site: Oakwood Elementary School.

In 1959, voters approved an $80,000 bond for Plymouth's first fire station with an all-volunteer crew. Captained by Chief Francis Bauer, pictured above, the nascent department had a rather infamous first call. On the night of December 28, 1959, they received a call to help the Brooklyn Park and Crystal Fire Departments with a house fire on Bass Lake Road. With minimal training, little equipment, and a borrowed truck, they started on their way, only to realize they had forgotten water! After backtracking to Wayzata, they arrived at the fire. Unfortunately, their pump would not work. While it was quite the misadventure, years later, they were able to laugh at the many lessons they learned that night. The photograph below captures two Plymouth Fire Department volunteers, Art and Loren Schiebe, inspecting a newly acquired smoke extractor in February 1963. (Below, courtesy of the Plymouth Fire Department.)

With its new designation as a village, Plymouth continued to expand services. In 1959, the city council approved the purchase of a fire siren and the distribution of "emergency call discs" printed with phone numbers for the Plymouth Fire and Police Departments. Plymouth's first full-time police officer was Claude Lien, who was named police chief in 1960. By 1967, the force had grown to include eight officers, pictured here. From left to right are Mike Woodward, Mel Solberg, Niel Nielsen, Claude Lien, Bruce Johnson, Harold Glampe, and Tom Tart. Outfitting the police force with the latest technology has evolved over the years. This 1978 Chevy Nova, pictured below, was prized at the time for its advanced options, including the attached speed radar. A neighboring community's department was less fortunate, their officers painting coffee cans black and attaching them to cars to resemble the Plymouth equipment. (Both, courtesy of the Plymouth Police Department.)

By 1972, the Luce Line was abandoned as a rail property and efforts were underway to convert it to a recreational trail. In July 1972, Plymouth council members passed a resolution encouraging the state to buy the Luce right-of-way for this purpose. Today, the Luce Line Trail is 63 miles long, stretching from Plymouth to Winstead. With diverse landscapes alternating between metropolitan and rural, the trail is enjoyed by bikers, hikers, horseback riders, and skiers. (Courtesy of the City of Plymouth.)

Plymouth's logo was unveiled on June 27, 1973, by (left to right) Councilmen John Spaeth and Marv Seibold, city engineer Sherm Goldberg, Mayor Al Hilde Jr., Councilman Gerry Neils, and city manager Jim Willis. The blue "P" stands for Plymouth, people, and planning, blue representing the community's commitment to clean water and air. Green leaves honor Plymouth's agricultural history and a pledge to protect outdoor recreation. The gear symbolizes Plymouth's diverse economic base, and the arrow represents the goal of a dynamic living space. (Courtesy of Howard Hunt.)

In 1972, Mayor Al Hilde Jr., pictured above, contacted local businessman Curt Carlson about organizing a free community music event. The objective was to create a definitive identity for Plymouth as a suburb with community pride and spirit. Carlson agreed to host the event in a vacant lot on his Minneapolis Industrial Park property. Nearly 8,000 people attended the first event in 1973, and "Music in Plymouth" was born as a beloved community tradition.

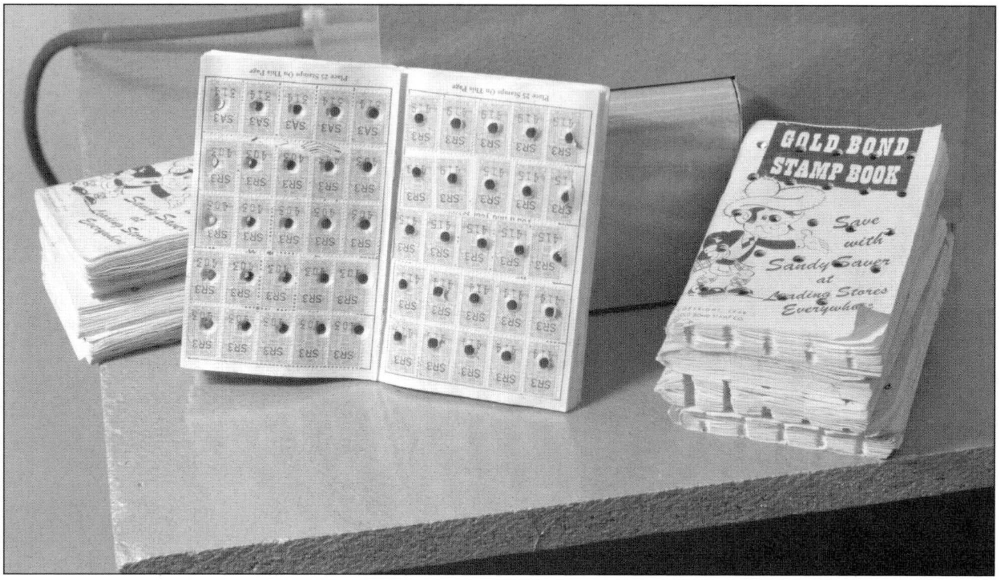

Curt Carlson founded the Gold Bond Stamp Company in 1938 with $55. Gold Bond Stamps were a consumer loyalty program in which stamps were collected and traded for items at grocery stores. The most popular prize was a four-slice toaster. As part of the early launch of his enterprise, Curt's wife, Arlene, would dress as a drum majorette, marching through stores lauding the stamps. As profits grew, Carlson continued to diversify his business, changing its name to Carlson Companies in 1973. By 1976, the company boasted an annual revenue of $1 billion. Carlson is pictured here to the right of Sen. Hubert Humphrey, Muriel Humphrey, and Bob Hope around 1975. (Both, courtesy of the Minnesota Historical Society.)

Florence Kardong watches Donna Heinitz sign the register at the first official meeting of the Plymouth Historical Society on November 12, 1975. Among those present were Mayor Henry Sahly and Niel Nielsen. Nielsen was the society's first president, Kardong was vice president, Debbie Yngve was secretary, and Maxine Haarstick was treasurer. Among the first goals of the fledgling group was securing the funding for the restoration of the old town hall, which had become an easily overlooked storage facility for the police department.

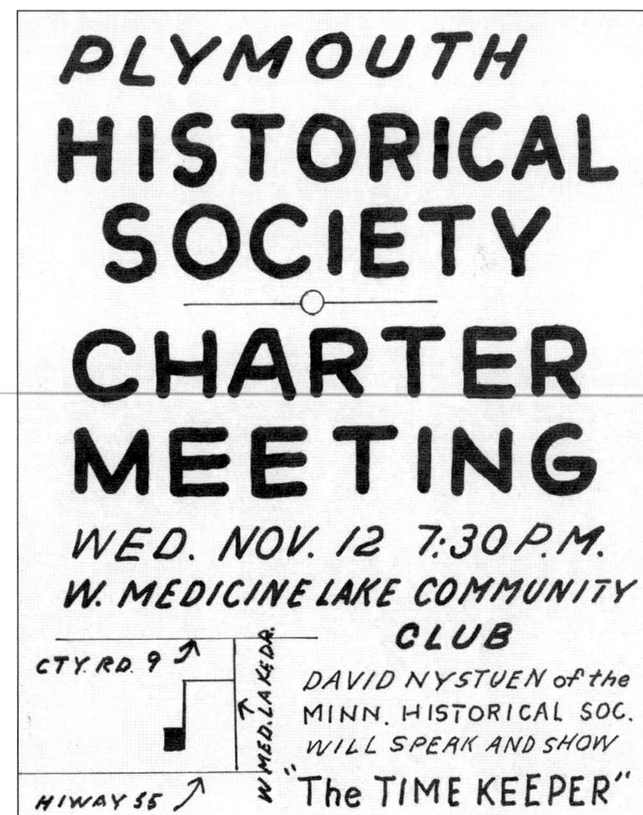

By the mid-1970s, Plymouth citizens began to realize the value of preserving the old town hall. Building and restoration efforts began, thanks, in part, to the efforts of police officer Niel Nielsen, who drove by it frequently while out on patrol. The building was moved back from Fernbrook Lane from its original fieldstone foundation to a new foundation in 1978, as seen in the photograph above. When the building was lifted, the stumps of trees cleared over one hundred years prior were revealed, along with several bottles and other artifacts. The photograph below shows a paint crew giving the old structure a new bright white façade. Around this time, the town hall was turned over to the Plymouth Historical Society as a place for the preservation of Plymouth's story.

On January 20, 1974, the Radisson Playhouse opened with a performance of *Play It Again, Sam*. The 211-seat theater was eventually renamed the Plymouth Playhouse in the early 1980s and came under the direction of Curt Wollan's Troupe America production company. Among the original productions performed by Troupe America were *The Church Basement Ladies* and the *How to Talk Minnesotan* series.

This 1975 aerial photograph shows the increasing urbanization of Plymouth along Xenium Lane. The familiar tower in the distance was constructed in the early 1970s for transmission of telephone and radio communication. At 310 feet, with its dark brown octagonal shapes, the tower was lauded as an "aesthetic landmark" in the October 1972 issue of the *Plymouth Voter*. (Courtesy of the City of Plymouth.)

By the late 1970s, Plymouth's population was nearing 30,000 residents, and the need was great for a new city hall. Mayor Al Hilde stands in the center of this photograph taken at the Plymouth City Center ground-breaking in 1978. The Plymouth City Center was designed with energy conservation in mind and was constructed with the help of an $82,000 Department of Energy grant. The City Center was dedicated on June 2, 1979. (Courtesy of Howard Hunt.)

In the late 1980s, after a portion of land belonging to the City of Minneapolis Workhouse was gifted to Plymouth, plans were made to develop Parkers Lake Park. This photograph captures the festive nostalgia incorporated into the ground-breaking ceremony for the park, which opened in 1987. Today, Parkers Lake Park features a boat launch, rentable park building, a picnic shelter, sand volleyball, and numerous trails.

Sometimes, evidence about the past shows up in the most unexpected places. This was certainly the case with Plymouth's earliest town records. In the summer of 1984, Niel Nielsen inspected this abandoned farmhouse (above) before it was burned in a training exercise by the Plymouth Fire Department. In the attic, Nielsen discovered a water-damaged wooden box containing the first two town clerk record books for Plymouth Township. The records were carefully dried out, and they now belong to the Plymouth Historical Society. Pictured below is the farmhouse when it belonged to Samuel Merchant in 1872. Merchant was one of Plymouth's earliest settlers, making his claim in September 1854.

For the city's 1976 bicentennial festivities, the Plymouth Lions Club held a "Plymouth Rock Contest," a rock beauty pageant of sorts. Vern Peterson's 300-pound rock was selected to become the Lions' new City Center monument. In 1980, the Lions' rock faced competition from a new Plymouth Rock contender: the 150-ton "Stadium Boulder," seen here lifted into place in front of First Bank's Four Seasons branch. (Courtesy of the Plymouth Police Department.)

The Plymouth Ice Center opened in 1996 as a public-private partnership between the City of Plymouth, Wayzata Public Schools, the Wayzata Youth Hockey Association, and Lifetime Fitness. The venture's success inspired other communities to follow this model. In 2004, a third sheet of ice was added, and the partnership expanded to include Providence Academy. The center hosts hockey, ice skating, speed skating, and broomball. (Courtesy of the City of Plymouth.)

Every winter since 1989, Plymouth has set winter ablaze during the Fire & Light Festival. Held at Parkers Lake, the festival mixes expected winter scenes (sled dogs, hayrides, snowshoeing) with unexpected ones (ice bowling, recycling bin races, treasure hunts). The grand finale is, of course, the fireworks. The event was started by Karol Gurepner and has had many contributors over the years, including the Plymouth Civic League and the Parks and Recreation Department. (Courtesy of the City of Plymouth.)

In 2008, *Money* magazine named Plymouth the "Best Place to Live in the Nation." This was followed by a resolution from the Minnesota State Senate applauding Plymouth for this recognition and its commitment to a high quality of life for its residents. The commendation noted the community's excellent schools, affordable housing, job opportunities, amenities such as the Hilde Performance Center, and events such as Music in Plymouth. (Courtesy of the City of Plymouth.)